MIMESIS
INTERNATIONAL

LITERATURE

n. 16

Alessio Mattana

DISCIPLINING THE IMAGINATION

Newtonianism and Prose Narrative in Eighteenth-Century Britain

MIMESIS
INTERNATIONAL

© 2024 – Mimesis International
www.mimesisinternational.com
e-mail: info@mimesisinternational.com

Isbn: 9788869774812
Book series: *Literature* n. 16

© MIM Edizioni Srl
P.I. C.F. 02419370305

CONTENTS

ACKNOWLEDGMENTS

The writing of this book, which has engaged me for the past two years, has racked up a number of debts. I am most grateful to Robert Jones, my doctoral supervisor, for his unfaltering guidance, and for teaching me the value of serious scholarship and perspicuous academic writing. For their suggestions and support, I also wish to thank the lecturing staff at the School of English of the University of Leeds, especially Richard De Ritter, whose advice was priceless, and Jeremy Davies and David Fairer, who were kind enough to share their erudition with me and encouraged me when I was still a postgraduate researcher.

I was fortunate enough to receive feedback from Gregory Lynall, who offered invaluable comments on this study when it was still a PhD thesis, and Geoffrey Cantor, who clarified some of my doubts about the finest points of Newtonianism. To both of them go my heartfelt thanks.

For their unwavering support over the years, I would like to thank the teaching staff at the Department of Foreign Languages at the University of Turin, especially Carmen Concilio, Pietro Deandrea and Virginia Pulcini, who have been instrumental to the success of my research endeavours.

I am forever indebted to Maria Grazia Dongu and Lucia Folena, two of my former English literature lecturers, for setting me on the path of eighteenth-century studies. It is thanks to their fascinating classes that I became enthralled by the literature and culture of early-modern England.

I benefited enormously from the company of Arianna Mazzieri, Laura Lucia Rossi, Giacomo Savani and Rachel Sulich. It is no overstatement to say that this monograph would not have existed were it not for their enlightening conversations and genial companionship.

INTRODUCTION

Disciplining the Imagination examines the relationship between Newtonianism and prose narrative in eighteenth-century Britain. The main argument made in this book is that prose narrative enacted, dramatized and problematized the confidence in human knowledge-making abilities which characterized eighteenth-century Newtonianism. Such confidence, I contend, was the long-lasting effect of Newton's ideas on British culture, one so widespread that it became common for thinkers in fields such as religion, moral philosophy and literature to seek certain principles in a manner akin to what Newton had allegedly done in natural philosophy. The requirement for determining phenomena with certainty, I also claim, was to adopt the *hypotheses non fingo* methodology Newton had formulated in his works, a belief which popularisers spread across eighteenth-century British culture in the form of what I call Newtonianism. The *hypotheses non fingo* required that observers restrain their imagination on the basis that subjective interpretations which are not backed by verifiable data corrupt observations, and thus impede a truthful assessment of a given phenomenon. This belief had momentous ramifications for prose narratives.

Disciplining the Imagination aims at making two key contributions to current scholarship. First, it offers a new theoretical perspective on the study of eighteenth-century culture. It claims that Isaac Newton's ideas were disseminated in British culture in the form of Newtonianism, a term used in this monograph to describe a two-fold cultural phenomenon. On the one hand, Newtonianism identifies the rich body of work produced in eighteenth-century Britain which overtly referenced Newton's ideas and his figure. Along with Newton's own oeuvre, this includes paratextual apparatus, translations of foreign commentaries on Newton, popularizations, periodical articles, literary works referencing Newton, and even inscriptions on his statues. A lesser-studied, yet complementary secondary sense of Newtonianism will also be introduced. In *Disciplining the Imagination*, Newtonianism will be understood as a climate of thought derived from the public attention given to Newton's figure and discoveries. Ideas initially related to Newton and disseminated through the body of work published on Newton were transformed and circulated to the point that they were no longer explicitly recognized as being derived from him. The main characteristic of this climate of thought, I will argue, was the confidence in the human ability to create knowledge with very high levels of certainty. Newton's own methodological statements in the *Principia* and the *Opticks* had emphasized that certainty in natural philosophy resulted from being uncompromising in seeking objective evidence. Hypotheses should always be discarded, as Newton believed them to be fictional aberrations produced by the imagination with no link to the reality of nature. Popularisers focused on this aspect of Newton's method and conveyed the need to discipline the observer's imagination as the essential condition of an accurate search into truth. Over time, I argue, this became an underlying epistemological assumption in eighteenth-century British culture.

Secondly, *Disciplining the Imagination* makes an empirical contribution within the history of British prose narrative by examining the works of a group of authors in close detail, analysing them vis à vis published scholarship and assessing to what extent they reacted to Newtonianism. The overarching claim made throughout this monograph is that writers used prose narrative as the choice medium to examine the epistemological ramifications of Newtonianism. In particular, I contend that the authors discussed in this book – Daniel Defoe, Henry Fielding and David Hume – used prose narrative to investigate how knowledge-making works in complex situations, exploring the possibility of stating things with certainty and debating the limits of the imagination. This claim, which is grounded on the argument that prose narrative in eighteenth-century Britain was not a finished product but an inchoate, experimental process, one in which the categories of romance, novel, history and biography tended to overlap and interact, also leads to a problematization of generic and disciplinary boundaries, especially the difference between fiction and non-fiction.

As explained in Chapter one, *Disciplining the Imagination* adopts a hybrid methodology which brings together close reading and intellectual history with the aim of highlighting the epistemological questions that are central to the book's argument. Close reading will be deployed to scrutinise the content of each source under the assumption that historical knowledge, as Peter De Bolla puts it, is always discursive because it is transmitted via written words, the oral element of history being irretrievably lost.[1] This is why close reading will be paired with an intellectual history approach, which ensures that the study of historical texts is situated within the intellectual and discursive contexts which authors sought to influence. Following Quentin Skinner, *Disciplining the Imagination* takes 'the performativity of texts and the need to treat them intertextually' as a point of departure for the analysis of all texts discussed in the monograph.[2]

In adopting this methodology, this work finds its niche in a current of publications arguing that in eighteenth-century Britain the boundaries between scientific and narrative practices were porous. Newton's ideas were conveyed in the same venues where literature was commented on. The connection of science and sociability was very strong in an age when scientific practice was the domain of gentlepeople of wide interests. Accordingly, alongside the printing press, the *loci* of the diffusion of Newtonianism were coffee-house conversations and public demonstrations.[3] Unsurprisingly, the writing of science and of literature tended to overlap, with

---

1   Peter De Bolla, *The Discourse of the Sublime: Readings in History, Aesthetics and the Subject* (Oxford: Blackwell, 1989), pp. 4, 7–8

2   Quentin Skinner, *Vision of Politics. Volume 1: Regarding Method* (Cambridge: Cambridge University Press, 2002), p. vii.

3   Richard Coulton, '"The Darling of the Temple-Coffee-House Club": Science, Sociability and Satire in Early Eighteenth-Century London', *Journal for Eighteenth-Century Studies*, 35 (2012), 43–65 (p. 44). On the printing press as an agent for the diffusion of Newton's ideas, see Laura Miller, *Reading Popular Newtonianism: Print, the* Principia, *and the Dissemination of Newtonian Science* (Charlottesville: University of Virginia Press, 2018).

the very advancement of natural philosophy and its progressive characterization into modern sciences often grounded in literary terms.[4] Moreover, as Jill Marie Bradbury has rightly remarked, forms such as the romance and the novel were not clearly distinguishable from each other, and they were often used as synonyms of the more inclusive category of 'history'.[5] Taking into account this continuity between science and literature practices in the eighteenth-century, *Disciplining the Imagination* also chooses to avoid establishing firm formal boundaries with regards to genres. The rationale for this flexible approach to generic and disciplinary division is the belief that in eighteenth-century Britain the distinction between works of fiction and non-fiction was fuzzy rather than binary. This, in turn, informs the choice of the broader concept of 'narrative' in this book, as opposed to more restricted terms such as 'fiction' or 'novel'.

Chapter one, titled 'Achieving Certainty: Newtonianism in Eighteenth-Century Culture', builds on relevant scholarship in the field of Newton studies to argue that Newton's scientific ideas were crucial to eighteenth-century British culture in terms of what Newton personally thought as well as of how commentators and popularisers disseminated the ideas contained in *Philosophiae Naturalis Principia Mathematica* (first edition published in 1687) and *Opticks* (1704) to the broader public. The result of this process is best understood as Newtonianism, a term that, although already used in scholarship, is here innovatively introduced as both the body of work by and on Newton and as a 'climate of thought' based on his ideas. In presenting Newton as a revolutionary thinker who had radically changed the way people understood the workings of the universe, British commentators claimed that a new age had

---

4   As Tita Chico argues, eighteenth-century scientific texts often made use of
     formal devices typical of literature, especially figures of speech like metaphors
     and genres like the dialogue. See Tita Chico, *The Experimental Imagination:
     Literary Knowledge and Science in the British Enlightenment* (Stanford:
     Stanford University Press, 2018). See also Courtney Weiss Smith, *Empiricist
     Devotions: Science, Religion, and Poetry in Early Eighteenth-Century
     England* (Charlottesville: University of Virginia Press, 2016).
5   Jill Marie Bradbury, 'New Science and the "New Species of Writing":
     Eighteenth-Century Prose Genres', *Eighteenth-Century Life*, 27 (2003), 28–
     51 (p. 29).

been reached, one in which anyone willing to determine any given matter with certainty could confidently do so by applying Newton's *hypotheses non fingo*, the popular motto added to the *General Scholium* in the second edition of the *Principia* (1713).

Chapter two, titled 'Beyond Natural Philosophy: The Confidence and Anxiety of Newtonianism', expatiates on the influence of Newton's methodology on fields other than natural philosophy, especially literature. The Newtonianist approach was couched on a distrust of the faculty of imagination, which allegedly produced unverifiable, fantastical explanations, and a marked reliance on reason, which manifested itself through accurate measuring and unbiased observation. The chapter proceeds to show that this Newtonianist confidence soon became so widespread that it generated new assumptions about knowledge-making. It was believed that a degree of certainty close to that allegedly attained by Newton in his scientific enquiries could be attained in non-scientific fields, provided that the faculty of imagination be bridled by not feigning conjectures. This resulted in a new confidence in the human ability to discover universal principles in fields other than natural philosophy, as well as in an anxiety that Newton's exceptionality had shed light on the inadequacy of human understanding.

Chapter three, titled 'The Uncertainty of Things: The Critique of Conjectures in Defoe's *A Journal of the Plague Year*', offers a fresh perspective on Defoe by examining *A Journal of the Plague Year* (1722) as a work which problematizes the belief that natural phenomena could be understood with any degree of certainty. Defoe retrospectively elaborates on the epistemological anxiety that had resulted from the Great Plague in 1665, representing it as a challenge to the Newtonianist assumption that natural phenomena could be fully understood and thus brought under control. In the *Journal*, Defoe offers a commentary on knowledge-making assumptions, pointing in particular to the erroneous conjectures made by both lay-people and physicians. Defoe's criticism, however, is tempered by the realisation that in a plague-stricken setting, no one can help using the faculty of imagination to come up with fanciful explanations, even if this results in misleading conclusions which may occasion a significant increase in the casualties.

Chapter four, titled 'Sagacious Doubt: Fielding's *Tom Jones* and the Problem of Deceitfulness', examines Henry Fielding's works, and in particular his novel *The History of Tom Jones, a Foundling* (1749), in terms of Fielding's position that universal principles in the behaviour of man may be established with a degree of assuredness similar to that allegedly boasted by natural philosophy. As it will be argued in this chapter, in the *Essay on the Knowledge of the Characters of Men* (1743), Fielding confidently asserts that while humankind is generally prone to fall for deception, a few sagacious people, equipped with superior observation abilities, are able to detect fraudulent appearances and discern the true nature of a person. This philosophical position, which resonated with the Newtonianist claim that sagacity was the ability of penetrating into nature's secrets, found its dramatic enactment in Fielding's prose fiction. In *Tom Jones*, characters are systematically inclined to be deceived. The omniscient narrator, by contrast, is able to conduct a quasi-scientific analysis of the behaviour of the characters in the novel, and engages in conversation with readers so as to educate them to a more sagacious reading of human actions, meant as the ability to be sceptical when faced with the appearance and words of people. In a satirical piece on natural philosophy which appeared on *The Covent-Garden Journal* (1752), however, it will finally be seen how Fielding was sceptical about the attainability of such an ideal outside the domain of fiction.

Chapter five, titled 'The Fictions of Ancient History: Hume's *History of England* and the Science of Man', contends that in the volumes on Saxon and Middle Ages of *The History of England* (1754–61) David Hume presents ancient history as a set of experiments to verify the universal principles about humankind he had elaborated in his philosophical works. Differently from the Tudor and the Stuart ages, treated by Hume in the initial four volumes of the *History*, in the volumes on the Saxon and Middle Ages the validity of the historical sources available is questioned due to their being adulterated by the imagination of ancient historians. As Hume contests the veracity of said accounts, he shifts the focus of the historian's craft from the study of influential men to the study of the human passions, which in his philosophical works he had identified as the basis of the 'science of man'. In doing so, the chapter argues, Hume attempts to develop a scientific approach to historiography which tries to exclude the vagaries of the will of the individual to focus on the universal laws governing human behaviour in society, claiming, in the process, a degree of certainty equal to that of mathematics-based sciences.

A few words are needed to clarify the reason for the inclusion of Hume's *History of England*, which might look like the odd item out given that Defoe and Fielding are traditionally (if summarily) classed as novelists. The rationale for this choice lies in the shared representational concerns between fiction writing and historiography in eighteenth-century Britain. It bears recalling that many of what we now define novels were actually presented as histories to the eighteenth-century public. Defoe's *A Journal of the Plague Year* and Fielding's *Tom Jones* are but two examples of this. The subtitle of Defoe's *Roxana: The Fortunate Mistress* (1724), for instance, was *A History of the Life and Vast Variety of Fortunes of Mademoiselle de' Belau*. Fielding's *Joseph Andrews* (1742) was originally published as *The History of the Adventures of Joseph Andrews and of his Friend Mr. Abraham Adams*. Samuel Richardson's *Clarissa* was subtitled *the History of a Young Lady* (1748). This was not just a marketing ploy to sell stories that felt authentic (although it was also that, of course). The term 'history' had marked narrative connotations; tellingly, in Samuel Johnson's *Dictionary of the English Language* (1755) it is both defined as 'a narration of events and facts delivered with dignity' and a 'narration; relation'.[6]

Everett Zimmerman has persuasively shown that, for all their differences in terms of topic, fiction and history were both perceived as instances of 'the human need to personalize the immensities of universal time' – i.e., providing narrative order to real or imagined events via a representation process.[7] The methods of prose fiction can be found in eighteenth-century 'non-fiction' genres such as sermons, essays, biography and philosophy. Indeed, in the eighteenth century these genres were understood by many as literature due to

---

6   Samuel Johnson, *A Dictionary of the English Language* (London: A. Millar and R. and J. Dodsley, 1755), 'History'.

7   Everett Zimmerman, *The Boundaries of Fiction* (Ithaca and London: Cornell University Press, 1996), pp. 21–22.

the presence of a significant 'aesthetic function'.[8] Conversely, history writing partook in what Homer Brown has called the 'irreducible heterogeneity of the discourses and forms that contribute to the institution of the English novel'.[9] History-like fiction such as that produced by Defoe and Fielding took place 'within a world of acknowledged history which must itself be recognized as a human construction'.[10] In a similar manner, historians proper, especially those like Hume who wrote within the tradition of Enlightenment history in opposition to the annalistic approach, also conceded the need to offer narrative order to the historical facts being told.[11] Therefore, as Hayden White claims, the commonsensical objection that historical events differ from fictional events in that they can be assigned a specific time-space location does not quite hold when examining eighteenth-century writing in Britain. At that time, the methods of the historiographer and of the writer of fiction overlapped, insofar as they used the term 'history' as shorthand for their aim to order disparate experiences in a narrative way which, in either case, has its defining characteristic in its allegedly being 'unalloyed by elements of fancy'.[12]

Finally, some notes about the nomenclature used in this book are necessary, especially with reference to two recurrent words: Newtonianism and science. The term Newtonianism has been chosen to avoid the ambiguities generated by 'Newton's philosophy' and 'Newtonian philosophy', the two expressions that were common in eighteenth-century Britain. Only in 1751 did d'Alembert and Diderot use 'Newtonianisme' as a synonym for 'Philosophie Newtonienne' in the *Encyclopédie* (1751-1772), but the term never gained traction in Britain. The English Short Title Catalogue does not list any results for 'Newtonianism' and the only occurrence in

---

8   J. C. Hilson, 'Hume: The Historian as a Man of Feeling', *Prose Studies: History, Theory, Criticism*, 3 (1980), 93–108 (p. 93).

9   Homer Brown, 'The Institution of the English Novel: Defoe's Contribution', *Novel: A Forum on Fiction*, 29 (1996), 299–318 (p. 300).

10   Zimmerman, p. 22.

11   Ibid.

12   Hayden White, 'The Fictions of Factual Representation', *Grasping the World: The Idea of the Museum*, ed. by Donald Preziosi and Claire Farago (Abingdon and New York: Routledge, 2018), pp. 22–34 (p. 22).

the Eighteenth-Century Collections Online is the 1777 translation of a letter of Pope Clement XIV to Francesco Algarotti, the author of *Sir Isaac Newton's Philosophy Explain'd for the Use of the Ladies* (1739). As discussed in Chapter one, in this work Newtonianism is used in two senses, which will be clearly marked up to avoid unnecessary confusion. The expressions with 'commentaries on' and 'texts on' (such as 'commentaries on Newton') stand to identify works that directly engage with, or unmistakably evoke, Newton; all other uses refer to Newtonianism as a climate of thought. The adjective 'Newtonianist' indicates the confidence in the possibility to produce knowledge as certain as that of Newton. The adjective 'Newtonian' is instead used in its standard contemporary meaning of 'relating to or arising from the work of Newton, esp. his physical or optical theories' (OED).

As for science, every student of early-modern culture is familiar with how slippery this term can be. In the long eighteenth century, the concept of science had no currency in the way it does for us. Following Latin usage, 'science' simply meant knowledge, and the word 'scientist' was yet to be invented – it was only in 1834 that geologist William Whewell coined the term in analogy with artist, on the basis that words like *savant* and philosopher felt too lofty to identify people concerned with natural and physical phenomena. In the period considered in this monograph, science fell within the domain of natural philosophy, that branch of philosophy which concerned itself with the study of natural bodies. Since the early 1640s, the first commentators of Lord Bacon also used the expression 'experimental philosophy', which codified the study of the natural world performed via experiments, and, more broadly, by collecting empirical data. But science as an organized activity with a well-defined scientific method was still in its infancy, and boundaries between disciplines were rather porous. Newton himself did not see great difference between the corpuscular theory we now class as chemistry and the alchemy that he so often practiced.[13] Nor was his astronomical knowledge ever too far removed from his study of

---

13   Betty Jo Teeter Dobbs, *The Janus Faces of Genius: The Role of Alchemy in Newton's Thought* (Cambridge: Cambridge University Press, 2003).

Biblical chronology.[14] For these reasons, commentators have tended to use the term 'early science' as an umbrella term for activities in the early-modern world which can be considered as the precursors of our science. Taking these caveats into account, in this monograph the word 'science' and related words such as 'scientist' or 'scientific' are occasionally used for reasons of practicality.

---

14   Rob Iliffe, *Priest of Nature: The Religious Worlds of Isaac Newton* (New York: Oxford University Press, 2019).

CHAPTER 1
ACHIEVING CERTAINTY
Newtonianism in Eighteenth-Century British Culture

1.1. *Making Sense of Newton's Legacy*

For the eighteenth-century Briton, there was a time before and
a time after Isaac Newton. Somerset poet and physician Samuel
Bowden was not alone in believing that 'immortal Newton' had
ushered in a new age of knowledge, one where:

> Sages now trust to Fairy Scenes no more,
> Nor venture farther, than they see the Shore:
> They build on Sense, then reason from th' Effect,
> On well establish'd Truths their Schemes erect;
> By these some new *Phaenomena* explain;
> And Light divine in ev'ry Process gain.[1]

Especially after his death, the veneration for Newton intensified so
much that it gave rise to a veritable 'apotheosis'.[2] At his majestic funeral
peers acted as pallbearers and his coffin was interred at Westminster
Abbey, the reserve of noblepersons, royals, and poets of the calibre
of Geoffrey Chaucer. This vicinity to poets was fitting, for a number
of them praised Newton and immortalised his achievements in their
verses. Just in the years around Newton's death, one can count several
such tributes. In *The Seasons* (1727), Scottish poet James Thomson,
who was educated at Edinburgh University where Newtonian science

---

1   Samuel Bowden, *A poem on the new method of treating physic* (London: S.
     Chandler, 1726), p. 8.
2   See Mordechai Feingold, *The Newtonian Moment. Isaac Newton and the
     Making of Modern Culture* (New York: The New York Public Library, 2004),
     p. 169.

was being taught, saw Newton as 'pure intelligence, whom God / To mortals lent to trace his boundless works / From laws sublimely simple'.[3] In *The Excursion* (1728), David Mallet, also a Scottish poet and friend to Alexander Pope, praised the 'great Newton! Britain's justest pride, / The boast of human race' for having discovered the law of universal gravitation, that 'spring of motion, this hid power infus'd / Through universal nature'.[4]

Newton's image as a divine creature who had shed light on nature's mysterious workings was one that made his countrymen proud – too proud perhaps, if one trusts Voltaire's backhanded compliment that Newton was 'the Hercules of a fabulous story' to whom 'the ignorant ascribed all the feats of the ancient heroes'.[5] The famous inscription on Newton's bust in the Temple of British Worthies in Stowe, designed by William Kent in 1734, characterized the Woolsthorpe philosopher as the one to whom 'the God of Nature made to comprehend all his Works; and from simple Principles to discover the Laws never known, and to explain the Appearances never understood, of this stupendous Universe'.[6] Newton's figure became increasingly well-known among the general public, and he would go on to become the Briton who sat for the most portraits and sculptures apart from royals. Medallions with his engraved profile – a privilege usually accorded to kings and queens – became prized objects for collectors.[7] His public image was so immaculate that it bordered on uncritical acceptance. As a *Grub Street Journal* author wrote with reference to Newton's *Chronology of Ancient Kingdoms Amended* (1728), a posthumous work in which Newton re-dated ancient history events by a retrospective analysis of the recession of

---

3   In David Fairer, 'James Thomson, *The Seasons*', *A Companion to Literature from Milton to Blake*, ed. by David Womersley (Oxford: Blackwell, 2001), pp. 284–290 (pp. 285–286).

4   David Mallet, *The Works of David Mallet* (London: A. Millar, and P. Vaillant, 1759), p. 101.

5   François-Marie Arouet de Voltaire, *Letters Concerning the English Nation* (London: C. Davis and A. Lyon, 1733), p. 96.

6   Quoted in Daniel Defoe, *A Tour Thro' the Whole Island of Great Britain*, 4 vols (London: S. Birt et al., 1748), I, 229.

7   For reference, Newton boasts an estimated 122 portraits and 109 sculptures. See Milo Keynes, *The Iconography of Sir Isaac Newton to 1800* (Suffolk: Boydell Press, 2005).

the equinoxes, the 'extraordinary fame and reputation of this great man in some arts and sciences, may probably induce persons to pay too great a deference to his opinion in others'.[8]

The importance of Newton for eighteenth-century British culture was enormous, but current scholarship does not seem to reflect that adequately. Historians of science and philosophy have long identified the centrality of Newton's scientific ideas for the development of philosophy in Britain and Europe.[9] Notwithstanding what Gregory Lynall calls the 'immense cultural impact' of Newton and his works during the eighteenth century, however, the question of his influence beyond the strictly scientific and philosophical domains remains something of an open question, with relatively few studies devoted to the topic.[10]

Literature has especially been overlooked, with very little being published on the topic after Marjorie Hope Nicolson's seminal *Newton Demands the Muse: Newton's Opticks and the Eighteenth Century Poets* (1946), a study which masterfully parsed out the influence of Newton's ideas on the imagination of Augustan poets. It was only recently that book-length studies provided Newton-related insight on the relationship between science and literature in eighteenth-century England. Lynall's *Swift and Science* examined Swift's *A Meditation upon a Broom-Stick*, *A Tale of a Tub*, and *Gulliver's Travels* in terms of the theological and political ramifications of Newtonianism they incorporated. Al Coppola's *The Theater of Experiment* contended

---

8 *Grub Street Journal*, Thursday, May 3, 1733; Issue 175.

9 The main reference work for the impact of Newton's ideas on philosophy is Robert E. Butts and John W. Davis, eds, *The Methodological Heritage of Newton* (Toronto: University of Toronto Press, 1970). See also Andrew Janiak, 'Newton's Philosophy', *The Stanford Encyclopedia of Philosophy*, ed. by Edward N. Zalta (Stanford: Stanford University, 2016) <https://plato.stanford.edu/archives/win2016/entries/newton-philosophy>.

10 Gregory Lynall, *Swift and Science: The Satire, Politics, and Theology of Natural Knowledge, 1690–1730* (Basingstoke and New York: Palgrave Macmillan, 2012), p. 15. On Newton's impact on British culture, see Feingold, *Newtonian Moment*, pp. 143–167; Patricia Fara, *Newton: The Making of Genius* (London: Pan Macmillan, 2002); Robert Iliffe, '"Is He Like Other Men?" The Meaning of the *Principia Mathematica*, and the Author as Idol', *Culture and Society in the Stuart Restoration: Literature, Drama, History*, ed. by Gerald Maclean (Cambridge: Cambridge University Press, 1995), pp. 159–178.

that a major factor in the rise of Newtonianism was the fact that experiments and scientific ideas were increasingly staged as spectacles akin to Restoration theatre plays. Courtney Weiss Smith's *Empiricist Devotions* brought together a wide range of texts – from sermons to treatises to journals – to argue that empiricism was inseparable from literary and religious concerns. Tita Chico's *The Experimental Imagination* explored how a wide array of textual technologies, such as tropes and literary language, worked to make experimental culture widely accessible to lay people. Finally, Laura Miller's *Reading Popular Newtonianism* analysed the reception of Newton's *Principia* based on the argument that print, authorship and editorial strategies facilitated the dissemination of Newtonianism.[11]

While all these studies have proven essential in charting the intersections between literature and science in eighteenth-century Britain, none of them investigated the relationship between Newton's ideas and writing in the way, for example, Gillian Beer's *Darwin's Plots* did for Victorian literature.[12] Given Newton's status as one of the most influential natural philosophers in eighteenth-century Britain, and the receptiveness of many eighteenth-century prose writers to both philosophical and every-day affairs, this research question is now a pressing affair.

Exploring the influence of Newton on eighteenth-century writing demands, first off, an investigation into Newton's popularity in broader culture. Historians of science have tended to assume that Newton's ideas were so intellectually potent that they progressively won over fellow philosophers and scientific practitioners, with consensus eventually trickling down to lay readers. This is the position taken, for example, by Richard S. Westfall in *Never at Rest* (1979), still the most comprehensive biography on Newton to date. According to Westfall, Newton was an exceptional mind who could find 'an ordered cosmos where only chaos appeared'; within a few decades, Westfall's argument goes, the greatest minds

---

11   On top of Chico, Lynall, Miller and Weiss Smith, all referenced above, see Al Coppola, *The Theater of Experiment: Staging Natural Philosophy in Eighteenth-Century Britain* (New York: Oxford University Press, 2016).

12   Gillian Beer, *Darwin's Plots: Evolutionary Narrative in Darwin, George Eliot and Nineteenth-Century Fiction* (London: Routledge, 1983).

in Europe welcomed the ideas of the *Principia* as the new orthodoxy in natural philosophy, and, over time, Newton's philosophy became increasingly accepted by the lay public.[13]

While fascinating, this view has some problems. For one, it builds on the assumption that the philosophy of Newton was a clearly identifiable object. It is debatable, however, whether the public agreed on, or even clearly understood, what Newtonian philosophy was. The term 'philosophy' appears in Newton's texts to refer to a very specific discipline, natural philosophy, whose language to Newton was the very sectorial one of advanced mathematics. The *philosophandi modo* (the 'mode of philosophising') advocated in the *Principia* is declaredly the enquiry on the mathematical principles that determine the physical forces constituting nature, for the whole point (and difficulty) of philosophy, Newton writes, 'seems to be to discover the forces of nature from the phenomena of motions and then to demonstrate the other phenomena from these forces'.[14] In the *Principia*, this translates into an exposition of problems, propositions and theorems through a combination of complex geometrical diagrams and forbidding equations. Newton's declared goal of offering 'a full explanation [...] of how to determine true motions from their causes, effects, and apparent differences, and, conversely, of how to determine from motions, whether true or apparent, their causes and effects' made his approach to philosophy largely inaccessible to his contemporaries.[15]

Nor did this state of affairs improve significantly with the first edition of *Opticks* (1704), Newton's enquiry into the nature of light and colour. Although more intelligible because written in English (in contrast with the dry scientific Latin of the *Principia*) and focused on actual experiments rather than abstract mathematical reasoning, *Opticks* stands in continuity with the *Principia* in terms

---

13   Richard S. Westfall, *Never at Rest: A Biography of Isaac Newton* (Cambridge: Cambridge University Press, 1980), pp. 1, 38–39, 472.

14   Isaac Newton, *Philosophiae Naturalis Principia Mathematica,* ed. by I. Bernard Cohen, trans. by Anne Whitman (Berkeley, Los Angeles, and London: University of California Press, 1999), p. 382.

15   Newton, *Principia*, p. 415.

of Newton's use of a physics-heavy variety of natural philosophy.[16] Like its predecessor, the *Opticks* presents natural philosophy as a field to be explored only through specific technical means – in this case, complex experiments with prisms, lenses and sunlight which proved very difficult to replicate even for expert practitioners, and whose results were to be validated mathematically.[17] Such a method is made clear from the very first paragraph of the book, in which Newton disclaims that 'My Design in this Book is not to explain the Properties of Light by Hypotheses, but to propose and prove them by Reason and Experiments'.[18] Accordingly, the series of experiments on light and colour in the *Opticks* are preliminarily grounded on a set of definitions and axioms stated at the beginning of the text.

If what Newton pursued may be defined as a philosophical project, it was one that proved hard to understand even for philosophers by trade. Even a high-standing philosopher like John Locke had to rely on help by Dutch polymath Christiaan Huygens, one of the few people in Europe skilful enough to tackle the mathematics of the *Principia*, to confirm the validity of Newton's calculations and, by extension, the philosophical claims he made. In this sense, and notwithstanding his influence on fellow philosophers, it is difficult to think of Newton as a philosopher in the way Locke himself was.[19] Differently to virtually all other major philosophers active in

---

16   Thomas Kuhn considers the *Principia* as the offshoot of the classical Aristotelian tradition of geometry and mathematics applied to natural phenomena such as the movement of planets; whereas the *Opticks*, although displaying elements of the mathematico-geometrical lineage, is derived from a tradition that Kuhn calls 'experimental' and that has its founding father in Lord Bacon. Thomas S. Kuhn, 'Mathematical vs. Experimental Traditions in the Development of Physical Science', *The Journal of Interdisciplinary History*, 7 (1976), 1–31.

17   The difficulty encountered by European natural philosophers to replicate Newton's experiments is discussed in Dennis Sepper, *Newton's Optical Writings: A Guided Study* (New Brunswick: Rutgers University Press, 1994); A. Rupert Hall, *All Was Light: An Introduction to Newton's Opticks* (London and New York: Clarendon Press, 1993).

18   Isaac Newton, *Opticks, or, a Treatise of the Reflections, Refractions, Inflections & Colours of Light*, ed. by I. Bernard Cohen (New York: Dover Publications, 1979), p. 1.

19   This point is made very convincingly in Bernard Cohen and George E. Smith, 'Introduction', *The Cambridge Companion to Newton*, first edition, ed. by I.

the long eighteenth century, British or otherwise, Newton was not primarily concerned with finding applications of his ideas outside of the sphere of physics. This, alongside a well-documented reluctance to engage in public debates, might be the reason why Newton constantly refrained from discussing his works with those who he deemed lacking in mathematical proficiency. That Newton wanted his ideas to be assessed only by other mathematical experts was very clear to the eighteenth-century reading public. It was widely known that the 'Great *Sir Isaac Newton*' had written the *Principia* 'for The Few: both the Manner and Matter of it placing it out of the Reach of the Generality even of Learned Readers'.[20]

When assessing Newton's intellectual legacy, it is thus crucial to keep in mind that only a handful of people in Europe were able to read the *Principia* when it was first published, and that the *Opticks*, while relatively easier to peruse, was not read extensively either.[21] In fact, hardly anything philosophical Newton wrote was read first-hand, other than the few digestible prose excerpts at the beginning and end of the *Principia* and the *Opticks*. Intriguingly, Newton's most widely read work was the *Chronology*, a work only tangentially related to the bulk of his scientific production.[22] Peter Jones raises a very sensible point when he comments on the question of what, in absence of proof to the contrary, even an omnivorous, philosophically-inclined reader like David Hume would have known first-hand of Newton's works: 'the Prefaces, Definitions

---

Bernard Cohen and George E. Smith (Cambridge: Cambridge University Press, 2002), pp. 1–32 (p. 2).

20   Benjamin Sarum, 'Preface', in Samuel Clarke, *Sermons* (London: W. Botham, 1730), p. iii. See also Fara, p. 5.

21   On the reception of *Opticks*, see Sepper, chapter 10; Hall, chapter 4; Marjorie Hope Nicolson, *Newton Demands the Muse: Newton's* Opticks *and the 18th Century Poets* (Princeton: Princeton University Press, 2016), chapter 1.

22   On Newton's *Chronology*, see Frank E. Manuel, *Isaac Newton, Historian* (Harvard: Harvard University Press, 1963); Mordechai Feingold, 'Isaac Newton, Historian', *The Cambridge Companion to Newton*, second edition, ed. by Rob Iliffe and George E. Smith (Cambridge: Cambridge University Press, 2016), 524–543; Anna Marie Roos, 'Taking Newton on Tour: The Scientific Travels of Martin Folkes, 1733–1735', *British Journal for the History of Science*, 50 (2017), 569–601 (p. 576); Alessio Mattana, '*Antiquitas non fingo*: Newton, the Moderns and the Science of Ancient History', *Journal for Eighteenth-Century Studies*, 43 (2020), 447–461.

and Axioms of *Principia*, together with the General Scholium, the Rules of Reasoning in Book III and Cotes's famous Preface in the second edition', alongside 'parts of the *Opticks*, but especially [...] the Queries appended to Book III'.[23] In this scanty collection of direct references, the longest and conceptually richest item is the preface to the second edition of *Principia* (1713), which was not even written by Newton but by his close assistant and book editor, Plumian Professor of Mathematics Roger Cotes.

As a matter of fact, 'all educated people' were 'generally familiar with Newton's work', as Nicholas Capaldi points out.[24] Such familiarity was largely due to indirect access to Newton's ideas, be it via popularisations, public demonstrations or coffee-house conversations. This mediated access was the rule. Most of the knowledge about Newton's scientific ideas was conveyed through texts that simplified his arguments and highlighted their importance beyond the sphere of natural philosophy. To give some proportion, the first edition of *Principia* had a print run of approximately 300 copies, many of which seem to have remained unsold. By contrast, William Whiston's *Sir Isaac Newton's Mathematick Philosophy More Easily Demonstrated* (1716) sold about 4,000 copies, more than ten times as much.[25] Newton's popularity appeared to be a function of the numerous texts that presented his ideas. Especially from the early eighteenth century onwards, the English book market was crowded with texts on Newton's discoveries, with varying degrees of faithfulness to the original and with different audiences in mind.

Commentators who had been close to Newton in his lifetime recognized that a balancing act between the expectations of the audience and fidelity to their master's philosophical beliefs was required, especially with regards to the centrality of mathematics in Newton's philosophy. Willem Jacob 's Gravesande, who authored

---

23   Peter Jones, *Hume's Sentiments: Their Ciceronian and French Context* (Edinburgh: Edinburgh University Press, 1982), p. 12.

24   Nicholas Capaldi, *David Hume: The Newtonian Philosopher* (Boston: Twayne Publishers, 1975), p. 55.

25   Stephen D. Snobelen, 'On Reading Isaac Newton's Principia in the 18th Century', *Endeavour*, 22 (1998), 159–163 (p. 163).

an *Introduction to Sir Isaac Newton's Philosophy* (1720), strove to faithfully represent 'Newton's Philosophy' as the mathematics-based natural philosophy advocated in the *Principia* and the *Opticks*.[26] While 's Gravesande's text was constructed as a detailed step-by-step commentary on Newton's mathematical arguments, most other commentaries were 'popularisations' – that is, watered-down versions of Newton's arguments written for an audience of relatively novice readers. In his 1716 popularisation, Whiston, a protégé of Newton, undertook the task of divulging 'in a more easy Method' the philosophical ideas of the 'Great Man', with the goal of bringing Newton's philosophy 'within the Reach and Comprehension of those, who are but indifferently perhaps exercis'd in the Mathematicks, and communicate the Knowledge thereof as far as may be'.[27] This goal was shared by Henry Pemberton's widely read *A View of Sir Isaac Newton's Philosophy* (1728), which attempted to convey the main takeaways from Newton's works to the general public on the grounds that there are 'more Admirers of your wonderful Discoveries, than there are Mathematicians able to understand the first two Books of your Principia'.[28]

Other popularisers were not as concerned with faithfulness to Newton's ideas and were ready to make drastic changes to accommodate the needs of lay readers. Newton was made palatable to the public of well-educated, yet unspecialised readers by suggesting that mathematics was not necessary to his philosophy, a claim unwarranted by Newton's works.[29] In John Harris's *Astronomical Dialogues* (1719), a work inspired by Fontenelle's *Entretiens sur la pluralité des mondes* (1686), the aristocratic lady

---

26 Willem Jacob 's Gravesande, *Mathematical elements of natural philosophy confirmed by experiments, or an introduction to Sir Isaac Newton's philosophy* (London: J. Senex, 1720), p. ii.

27 William Whiston, *Sir Isaac Newton's Mathematick Philosophy More Easily Demonstrated* (London: J. Senex, 1716), p. 1. See James E. Force, *William Whiston, Honest Newtonian* (Cambridge: Cambridge University Press, 2002).

28 Henry Pemberton, *A View of Sir Isaac Newton's Philosophy* (London: S. Palmer, 1728), pp. 19–20.

29 On how popularisers divested Newtonian philosophy of mathematics to make it more palatable to the general public, see Alessio Mattana, 'The Modest Genius: Mathematics, Certainty, and the Creation of the Public Newton', *Eighteenth-Century Life*, 47 (2020), 30–62.

taking science lessons is 'frighted and deterred from beginning with *Geometry*, and the *abstracted Mathematicks*', but is assured by her gentleman tutor that even she can still learn the secrets of Newtonian philosophy as long as mathematics is expunged from explanations.[30] In the influential English translation of a similar work, Francesco Algarotti's *Il Newtonianismo per le Dame*, the narrator chooses to avoid mathematical terms and figures altogether, in spite of their importance in the *Principia* and the *Opticks*, so that the marchioness can master the gist of Newton's discoveries.[31]

1.2. *The Two Meanings of Newtonianism*

This 'distillation' of Newton's ideas into broader society (to borrow Laura Miller's phrase) allowed people to talk of Newtonian philosophy while sidestepping the complexity of Newton's works. It was a necessary process because, while Newton's popularity had been soaring among polite lay readers, who partook in the national pride for a man who they thought had single-handedly brought about a revolution in the study of nature, these same readers did not wish, nor thought it desirable, to delve into the mathematical complexities of the *Principia* or the *Opticks*.[32]

How did Newton's ideas come to be of interest for a community of people that, albeit well-read and educated, had little mathematical background? This problem might be helpfully reframed by looking at Massimo Mazzotti's contention that Newton's science did not exist

---

30   John Harris, *Astronomical Dialogues between a Gentleman and a Lady* (London: Benj. Cowse, 1719), p. 147.

31   Francesco Algarotti, *Sir Isaac Newton's Philosophy Explain'd for the Use of the Ladies. In Six Dialogues on Light and Colours* (London: E. Cave, 1739), pp. vi–vii. On the impact of Algarotti's text in Britain, see Laura Miller, 'Publishers and Gendered Readership in English-Language Editions of *Il Newtonianismo per le Dame*', *Eighteenth-Century Culture*, 42 (2013), 191–214.

32   Miller, 'Publishers and Gendered Readership', p. 197. On the eighteenth-century perception of Newton's work as having started an intellectual revolution, see I. Bernard Cohen, *The Newtonian Revolution* (Cambridge: Cambridge University Press, 1983), pp. 3–38.

in isolation from the culture in which it arose.[33] Thanks to a network of indefatigable, influential friends, Newton's ideas were circulated as a matter of the utmost public relevance from the very first moment, not lastly by literary means. It is telling that astronomer Edmond Halley, after convincing Newton to publish the *Principia*, went at great lengths to premise it with a Latin ode, whose translation reads 'Ode on This Splendid Ornament of Our Time and Our Nation'. Halley's poem was a panegyric in verses in which the discovery of the laws of the universe is cast as Newton's ever-lasting gift to the whole of humankind.[34] That of Halley was one of the very first steps in a cultural process aptly called by Larry Stewart 'the formation of consensus' over Newton's 'lasting reputation in the wider society', an operation that, over time, made the first-hand understanding of Newton's own words more and more unnecessary since his fame warranted the truthfulness of his claims.[35] As the Dissenter preacher Thomas Morgan put it, 'there are few thinking, inquisitive Persons, now among us, but know something of the *Newtonian* Philosophy, and the Laws of Nature demonstrated by that great Philosopher; but the Generality receive it only upon Trust'.[36]

To be sure, Newton did not reject this treatment while still alive. He nurtured his own myth assiduously, as Rob Iliffe, Simon Schaffer and Steven Shapin have variously shown.[37] Iliffe in particular has demonstrated how, by gate-keeping access to his texts and his own

---

33 Massimo Mazzotti, 'Newton for Ladies: Gentility, Gender and Radical Culture', *British Journal for the History of Science*, 37 (2004), 119–146 (p. 121).

34 Edmund Halley, 'Ode on This Splendid Ornament of Our Time and Our Nation', in Isaac Newton, *Philosophiae Naturalis Principia Mathematica*, ed. by I. Bernard Cohen, trans. by Anne Whitman (Berkeley, Los Angeles, and London: University of California Press, 1999), pp. 379–380.

35 Larry Stewart, *The Rise of Public Science: Rhetoric, Technology, and Natural Philosophy in Newtonian Britain, 1660–1750* (Cambridge: Cambridge University Press, 1992), p. xxix.

36 Thomas Morgan, *The Moral Philosopher. Vol. III. Superstition and Tyranny Inconsistent with Theocracy* (London: n.p., 1740), p. 126.

37 Iliffe, 'Is He Like Other Men?', pp. 159–160, 175; Simon Schaffer, 'Newton on the Beach: The Information Order of *Principia Mathematica*', *History of Science*, 47 (2009), 243–276 (pp. 243–247); Steven Shapin, '"The Mind Is Its Own Place": Science and Solitude in Seventeenth-Century England', *Science in Context*, 4 (1990), 191–218 (pp. 194, 205–206).

person, Newton was able to cultivate the pose of a virtuous person uninterested in the accolades of society because too engrossed in the discovery of the secrets of nature to care. Public acknowledgments were, however, far from irrelevant for Newton, who became President of the Royal Society in 1703, then Knight and Master of the Mint immediately afterwards. His social presence was elephantine by design, and the ostracization of Robert Hooke and John Flamsteed, the repeated attacks on the French supporters of Descartes and the vitriolic controversy with Leibniz on the invention on calculus all testify to Newton's ability to systematically take advantage of his status to undermine his detractors and bolster his primacy among European intellectuals.[38]

These disputes excited the imagination of Newton's countrymen, for whom subtleties in natural philosophy or experimental apparatus were largely irrelevant, but who were ready to side with the intellectual heroes of the day, as long as they carried the standard of British primacy. As Geoffrey Cantor succinctly puts it, 'superficiality' was what the motley audience of English-speaking readers seemed to require from Newton-related knowledge: ever so ardent to be acquainted about Newton's discoveries and talk about them, the public did not feel the need to master such knowledge to a degree higher than what simple conversation required.[39]

This helps us understand why newspapers and books were increasingly replete with references to a supposed 'Newton's philosophy' or 'Newtonian philosophy', though relatively few people were acquainted with the sources, nor were they interested in reading them first hand. A further layer of complexity is added by the fact that these expressions often concealed attempts to claim Newton's ideas for specific religious and political agendas. Margaret C. Jacob famously identified the proponents of Newtonian philosophy with a group of Whig low-church Latitudinarian thinkers who stood in

---

38   See John Bennett Shank, *The Newton Wars and the Beginning of the French Enlightenment* (Chicago: Chicago University Press, 2008), especially chapter seven.
39   Geoffrey N. Cantor, *Optics After Newton: Theories of Light in Britain and Ireland, 1704–1840* (Manchester: Manchester University Press, 1983), p. 46.

support of the king after the 1688 settlement.[40] The Newtonians, as Jacob famously called them, developed the religious implications in Newton's scientific ideas into a theological framework which was said to have been endorsed by Newton himself. Starting with the 1692 Boyle Lecture delivered by clergyman Richard Bentley, the Newtonians argued that the discovery of universal gravitation had shown that the cosmos was a harmonious system managed by an omnipresent and benevolent God. In their eyes, Newton's scientific ideas on a universe governed by a limited set of laws of motions contributed to the stabilisation of a society that, in the aftermath of the Glorious Revolution of 1688, was in dire need of cohesion.[41] In a 'universe desperate for stability', as Stewart puts it, Newton's laws of nature 'had meaning for theologians and for politicians who had need to control those social forces that had already unleashed a regicidal civil war' – a fact which, Stewart concludes, no person grown after the Restoration could ignore.[42]

Yet, that of the Boyle lecturers was only one of the possible appropriations of Newton's scientific ideas. Tory, High-Church Jacobites would also, and in good faith, claim to be keen adherents of the Newtonian philosophy.[43] Even radical texts that openly questioned traditional structures of religion and bordered on atheism, such as John Toland's *Letters to Serena* (1704), hinted at what they believed were the tenets of Newtonian philosophy.[44] At a time when the Parliament was becoming more and more influential in British politics, debates on the legitimacy of monarchical rule would also draw on Newton's ideas, as in the case of an anonymous

---

40   Margaret C. Jacob, *Newtonians and the English Revolution 1689–1720* (Ithaca: Cornell University Press, 1976). See also John Gascoigne, 'From Bentley to the Victorians: The Rise and Fall of British Newtonian Natural Theology', *Science in Context*, 2 (1988), 219–256.

41   Jacob, *Newtonians*, p. 73.

42   Stewart, p. 30.

43   Anita Guerrini, 'The Tory Newtonians: Gregory, Pitcairne, and their Circle', *Journal of British Studies*, 25 (1983), 288–311 (pp. 289–90, 311).

44   On John Toland's use of Newton's ideas, see Jeffrey R. Wigelsworth, 'Lockean Essences, Political Posturing, and John Toland's Reading of Isaac Newton's *Principia*', *Canadian Journal of History*, 38 (2003), 521–535. For an overview on Newton and religion, see James E. Force and Richard Popkin, eds, *Newton and Religion: Context, Nature and Influence* (Dordrecht: Springer, 1999).

1728 poetic satire in which ideas of natural order from the *Principia* were interpreted as validation for the kingdom of George II.[45]

This is to say that the amount and diversity of eighteenth-century references to Newtonian philosophy and Newton's philosophy is not a by-product, but one of the chief characteristics of the way Newton's ideas were spread in eighteenth-century Britain. As Anita Guerrini puts it, although not 'quite all things to all men', Newtonian philosophy was certainly not 'a coherent ideology outside the realms of science'.[46] People of variegated political and religious allegiances called themselves Newtonians with little need to show their scientific credentials; most importantly, they were just accepted as such. Newton's intellectual legacy, in an important sense, was very much up for grabs to whoever was willing to be perceived as Newtonian, regardless of their actual mastery of the natural philosopher's ideas.

Acknowledging this state of affairs leads to two complex questions: how did this fragmented landscape of references come to life? And is there a shared, defining characteristic in the references to Newton and his ideas which may be identified? In order to tackle these two questions, this book adopts the term 'Newtonianism', and its related adjective 'Newtonianist', to identify a complex cultural phenomenon which is best understood in two complementary senses, a strong and a weak one. Firstly, Newtonianism identifies the extensive body of texts that overtly referenced either Newton or his ideas in the long eighteenth century. Alongside Newton's own oeuvre, it includes paratextual apparatus within his works, such as Halley's *Ode* at the beginning of the first edition of *Principia* and Cotes' *Editor's Preface* attached to its second edition; popularisations like Pemberton's *A View of Sir Isaac Newton's Philosophy* and Colin MacLaurin's *An Account of Sir Isaac Newton's Philosophical Discoveries* (1748); the many newspaper articles on Newton's achievements and personal qualities; literary works which nominated Newton, such as, for instance, Alexander Pope's *An Essay on Man* (1733); and, in a broader sense, non-literary works such as monuments, sculptures and inscriptions about Newton – as, for example, the statue in

---

45   David J. Twombly, 'Newtonian Schemes: An Unknown Poetic Satire from
      1728', *British Journal for Eighteenth-Century Studies*, 28 (2005), 251–272.
46   Guerrini, p. 311.

Westminster Abbey – and even paintings and medallions depicting Newton or containing Newton-inspired imagery.

The second, weaker sense of Newtonianism is much more evasive, but essential to appreciating how the ramifications of Newton's ideas found their way into literary works. In a century when, in the words of Fara, 'generations of interpreters' created their 'mythical visions of Newton from which the central core of the man himself is missing', the historiography of cause-effect relations can only go so far in providing a full sense of the extent and pervasiveness of Newton's intellectual influence in British culture.[47] Like some of the major thinkers in the history of humankind, Newton embodies the paradox of an enormously popular author whose works were rarely read. The transmission of his image and his ideas on nature transformed eighteenth-century thought in ways that are difficult to trace because they run deeper than straightforward cause-effect relationships. To navigate this fluid scenario, it is vital to go beyond what John R. R. Christie calls 'the stubborn empirical streak in Anglo-American historiography' – that is, the establishment of direct influences between authors – and look for other clues to complement any external evidence we may find.[48]

The second meaning of Newtonianism proposed in this book is thus that of an 'intellectual climate' (a term that will be used interchangeably with 'climate of thought'). Within this intellectual climate, ideas initially related to Newton were constantly transformed and re-circulated to the point that they were not necessarily recognized as being derived from him. The mechanics of Newtonianism as a climate of thought proposed in this book are analogous to those investigated by De Bolla in his *The Discourse of the Sublime* (1989), where it is argued that the thousands of texts on the topic of the sublime that were published in the second half

---

47 Fara, p. xv. On the constructed mythology of Newton's biographies see Michael Fores, 'Constructed Science and the Seventeenth Century "Revolution"', *History of Science*, 22 (1984), 217–244.

48 John R. R. Christie, 'Introduction: Rhetoric and Writing in Early Modern Philosophy and Science', *The Figural and the Literal: Problems of Language in the History of Science and Philosophy, 1630–1800*, ed. by Andrew E. Benjamin, Geoffrey N. Cantor, John R. R. Christie (Manchester: Manchester University Press, 1987), pp. 1–9 (p. 1).

of the eighteenth century engendered a discourse of the sublime. This discourse acquired an existence that was independent from the publications on the topic, up to the point that people started to think in terms of the 'sublime' even if they were not necessarily acquainted with the relevant works published on the topic.

De Bolla's study of the sublime adopts an empirically weak approach to history, and this is precisely where its explanatory power lies. Enquiries into the distant past, as De Bolla contends, carry with them the almost insurmountable difficulty of 'talking at the most general levels about the subject and history'. Because of our very standpoint as situated observers with no direct evidence of things past, we must accept that our historical analyses of the eighteenth century are textually mediated, for they necessarily deal with 'the aims and intentions of dead persons' to whom we no longer have direct access. Whatever our trust in historical sources, 'historical knowledge is, de facto, discursive' because it is transmitted to us via written words, and the oral part is completely lost. Rather than looking for an irretrievable authorial intention, the historian of thought should thus devote their energies to the recognition of those discursive networks that 'articulate the real' – that is, the imaginative ways through which historical actors represented their own world.[49]

This approach, which is inspired by that adopted by the French historiographers of the *Annales* School, allows one to look for traces of Newton's ideas even where evidence of first-hand readings of Newton is missing or fragmentary.[50] Newtonianism, in other words, manifests itself not just as a body of texts on Newton and his ideas, but also as an ethereal influence on the way people thought as well.

---

49   De Bolla, pp. 4, 7–8. It bears adding that in its original Foucauldian sense, the word 'discourse' is charged with meta-epistemological questions that are not necessarily at play here. This is apparent, for instance, in *The Order of Things*, where Foucault claims to be interested in understanding how 'knowledge and theory became possible; within what space of order knowledge was constituted'. Michel Foucault, *The Order of Things: An Archaeology of the Human Sciences*, trans. by Tavistock/Routledge (London and New York: Routledge, 1989), p. xxiii.

50   For a brief overview on the French historiography of mentality, see Alfred J. Andrea, 'Mentalities in History', *The Historian*, 53 (1991), 605–608. On the global impact of the Annales school, see Peter Burke, 'The "Annales" in Global Context', *International Review of Social History*, 35 (1990), 421–432.

In effect, this means that Newtonianism must also be 'inferred'. As Richard Striner puts it:

> The Newtonian paradigm may at times be traced through intellectual biography as well as through source analysis for establishing doctrinal provenance. But it must also be inferred from a long-vanished netherworld of dinner parties at which no Boswell served as recording angel, from continuing chatter through which ideas might be picked up at third and fourth hand and become absorbed into the ruminative life of individuals.[51]

Newton's ideas, mediated by a steady stream of commentaries, seeped into what Striner calls 'the ruminative life of individuals' – that is, the way people digested ideas and made them into their own, creating a climate of opinion that, while affected by the texts published on Newton, was not limited to them. With traces of Newton's ideas being scattered, fragmented and re-purposed all the time, often without a clear perception of their being derived from either Newton or his commentators, the literary scholar thus needs to look at the way eighteenth-century writing might have assimilated Newton's ideas in indirect ways as well as direct ones.

1.3. *Newton's Quest for Certainty and its Epistemological Ramifications*

The second question that needs to be addressed in relation to Newtonianism is whether a shared, defining characteristic may be identified. Evidence suggests that, while references to Newton were quite heterogeneous, Newtonianism had one defining feature in the idea that a new standard for knowledge-making had been set after Newton. Not only was Newton regarded as the culmination of centuries of intellectual progress; he was also believed to have shown that the secrets of nature could be understood with the

---

51　Richard Striner, 'Political Newtonianism: The Cosmic Models of Politics in Europe and America', *The William and Mary Quarterly*, 52 (1995), 583–608 (p. 584).

certainty of mathematical demonstration rather than by means of speculative hypotheses.

In eighteenth-century Britain, the name 'Newton' and the adjective 'Newtonian' came to codify the belief that knowledge of nature was no longer tentative, for it had been found that all natural phenomena were governed by a limited set of invariable laws.[52] As populariser Benjamin Martin explained, Newton's system 'of plain and genuine Truth' is made up of principles that 'naturally tend to correct our Senses, to improve our Reason, to enlarge our Understanding, to illumine the Mind, and raise the Soul to the highest Pitch of rational Knowledge our Nature will admit of in this earthly State'.[53] Or, as eloquently written by an anonymous mid-century periodical writer:

> [Newton's] account of the Universe and the laws by which it is regulated, is founded upon the most indubitable principles of Reason, Science, and Observation. We are now, no longer, to wander through the intricate mazes of hypothesis and conjecture. Nature appears again, in all her primitive simplicity. Newton has dissolved the chaos, and separated the light from the darkness.[54]

It was widely believed that Newton had ushered in a new era of knowledge-making, one in which humankind was no longer to wander through a labyrinth of uncertain speculations. As long as his method was replicated, the argument went, one could identify laws and principles with the certainty of Newton, not just in natural philosophy but in other fields as well. This confidence became widespread and characterized Newtonianism as a climate of thought for the entire eighteenth century, finding its way in literary works too in various guises, as it will be shown in the next chapters.

---

52   Rienk Vermij, 'The Formation of the Newtonian Philosophy: The Case of the Amsterdam Mathematical Amateurs', *British Journal for the History of Science*, 36 (2003), 183–200 (p. 183).

53   Benjamin Martin, *A Panegyrick on the Newtonian Philosophy. Shewing the Nature and Dignity of the Science, and Its absolute Necessity to the Perfection of Human Nature; the Improvements of Arts and Sciences, the Promotion of true Religion, the Increase of Wealth and Honour, and the Completion of Human Felicity* (London: W. Owen, 1769), p. 8.

54   *Adventurer*, Tuesday, March 5, 1754; Issue 139.

Crucially, this new era in knowledge-making had been made possible by Newton's rejection of the faculty of imagination. The roots of this claim may be found in Newton himself, who stressed that striving for mathematical certainty when investigating natural phenomena demanded that the observer's imagination be kept in check. The first traces of this approach may be found in a letter, which came to be known as 'New Theory about Light and Colors', that Newton sent to the Royal Society in 1672 to describe his prismatic experiments.[55] In a paragraph later removed by the editor of the *Philosophical Transactions*, Newton maintains he would not 'mingle conjectures with certainties' when examining the behaviour of light and colour:

> A naturalist would scarce expect to see the science of those [colours] become mathematicall, & yet I dare affirm that there is as much certainty in it as in any other part of Opticks. ffor what I shall tell concerning them is not an Hypoth{esis} but most rigid consequence, not conjectured by barely infer{ring} 'tis thus because not otherwise or because it satisfies all phænomena (the Philosophers universall Topick,) but evinced by the mediation of experiments concluding directly & without any suspicion of doubt.[56]

Newton's position about imagination-based conjectures remained the same throughout his life. As Alan Shapiro explains, he continued to pursue his goal to claim 'a greater degree of certainty than most

---

55 Isaac Newton, 'New Theory about Light and Colors', *Philosophical Transactions of the Royal Society*, 80 (1672), 3075–3087 (p. 3085). On the editorial vicissitudes of this letter, see Zev Bechler, 'Newton's 1672 Optical Controversies: A Study in the Grammar of Scientific Dissent', *The Interaction Between Science and Philosophy*, ed. by Yehuna Elkana (New Jersey: Humanities Press, 1974), pp. 115–142.

56 Isaac Newton, *MS Add. 3970.3* (Cambridge: Cambridge University Library), f. 462v. See Stephen Gaukroger, 'Empiricism as a Development of Experimental Natural Philosophy', *Newton and Empiricism*, ed. by Zvi Biener and Eric Schliesser (New York: Oxford University Press, 2014), pp. 15–38 (p. 26); Mordechai Feingold, 'Mathematicians and Naturalists: Sir Isaac Newton and the Royal Society', *Isaac Newton's Natural Philosophy*, ed. by Jed Z. Buchwald and I. Bernard Cohen (Cambridge: MIT, 2001), pp. 77–101 (p. 83).

of his contemporaries allowed'.[57] The *Principia* and the *Opticks* were carefully planned applications of this goal, both displaying a sharp demarcation between conjectures and what Newton variously defines as demonstrative, certain and true knowledge.[58] This is especially evident in the description of the 'method of analysis' included in the long Query 31 of *Opticks* (originally part of the 1706 Latin edition *Optice* and translated in English in 1717 for a revised edition), where hypotheses are opposed to 'experiments, or other certain Truths':

> This Analysis consists in making Experiments and Observations, and in drawing general Conclusions from them by Induction, and admitting of no Objections against the Conclusions, but such as are taken from Experiments, or other certain Truths. For Hypotheses are not to be regarded in experimental Philosophy. [...] And if no Exception occur from Phaenomena, the Conclusion may be pronounced generally.[59]

In Query 28, this distinction is further elaborated on via an attack against unnamed 'philosophers', most likely Descartes and his French followers, who subscribed to the theory of vortices to explain attraction between bodies. These philosophers, Newton alleges, kept on 'feigning hypotheses for explaining all things mechanically, and referring other Causes to Metaphysicks', whereas the 'main Business of natural Philosophy is to argue from Phaenomena without feigning Hypotheses'.[60]

Newton was adamantine in his belief that certainty could be achieved in knowledge-making processes as long as the observer

---

57   Alan E. Shapiro, *Fits, Passions, and Paroxysms: Physics, Method, and Chemistry and Newton's Theories of Colored Bodies and Fits of Easy Reflection* (Minnesota: University of Minnesota Press, 2009), p. 14.

58   The 'Queries' section in *Opticks* is the most glaring instance of this organising principle. Annexed to the end of the volume, Newton employs the 'Queries' to freely entertain, and comment on, suppositions on various subjects (including alchemy) without them interfering with the theory of colours and light presented in the main body of *Opticks*. Shapiro argues that Newton distinguished between 'experimental' and 'imaginary hypotheses', making use of the former and discarding the latter, but it is worth noting that Newton never makes this distinction explicitly. See Shapiro, p. 17.

59   Newton, *Opticks,* p. 404.

60   Newton, *Opticks*, p. 369.

was able to avoid imaginative explanations. This position would find its motto in the General Scholium to the second edition of *Principia* published in 1713, where the famous *hypotheses non fingo* motto is first stated. The motto, which translates as 'I do not feign hypotheses', brings together the semantic sphere of hypothesis-making with that of fiction via the verb *fingere*, from which the noun *fictio* derives.[61] Hypotheses are the product of the imagination, and imagination is, in turn, a faculty that adulterates the data provided by 'the evidence of experiments'. Using one's imagination, Newton writes, is to 'depart from the analogy of nature', hypotheses being subjective explanations with no necessary link to what nature actually displays. If one truly wants to understand natural phenomena, conjectures are to be refrained from.[62]

In effect, this means that observers of nature need to drastically restrain their tendency to interpret nature. In Newtonian terms, a natural phenomenon is a self-evident expression of nature that does not require further elaboration as long as it is mathematically computable. As Peter Achinstein explains, phenomena in this respect are not simple secondary qualities perceived by the senses (the then-commonly accepted philosophical meaning of the term) but 'noncontroversial' entities, facts that are beyond dispute.[63] The 'basic problem of philosophy', Newton argues, is not finding explanations for the mysteries of nature – which would require a leap of the imagination, i.e., hypotheses – but to 'discover the forces of nature from the phenomena of motions and then to demonstrate the other phenomena from these forces'.[64] It is in this sense that Newton, in a seemingly self-contradictory passage, maintains that his

---

61   I. Bernard Cohen, 'The First English Version of Newton's Hypotheses Non Fingo', *Isis*, 53 (1962), 379–388 (p. 381).

62   Newton, *Principia*, p. 795.

63   Peter Achinstein, 'Newton's Corpuscular Query', *Philosophical Perspectives on Newtonian Science*, ed. by Phillip Bricker and R. I. G. Hughes (Cambridge and London: The MIT Press, 1990), pp. 135–174 (p. 138).

64   Newton, 'Author's Preface to the Reader', in Isaac Newton, *Philosophiae Naturalis Principia Mathematica*, ed. by I. Bernard Cohen, trans. by Anne Whitman (Berkeley, Los Angeles, and London: University of California Press, 1999), pp. 381–383 (p. 382).

'principles of philosophy' are 'not, however, philosophical but strictly mathematical'.[65]

As long as they are not adulterated by the observer's imagination, phenomena are for Newton objective enough for universal laws to be elicited from them. The discovery of causes derived from an impartial observation of phenomena is what in *Opticks* is called the 'method of analysis', which proceeds 'in general, from Effects to [...] Causes, and from particular Causes to more general ones, till the Argument ends in the most general'. Analysis is then followed by what Newton calls 'method of synthesis', which 'consists in assuming the Causes discover'd, and establish'd as Principles, and by them explaining the Phaenomena proceeding from them, and proving the Explanations'.[66] This same pattern of analysis and synthesis can be identified in the third and the fourth rule of reasoning in *Principia*. Rule 3, which states that 'those qualities of bodies [...] that belong to all bodies on which experiments can be made should be taken as qualities of all bodies universally', generalizes phenomenal patterns into universally valid laws. Accordingly, in Newton's own commentary to Rule 3, the law of universal gravitation is said to have been established by 'experiments and astronomical observations'.[67] Rule 4 clarifies that hypotheses can never be used as evidence. Only a careful observation of phenomena can be used to produce certain knowledge:

> In experimental philosophy, propositions gathered from phenomena by induction should be considered either exactly or very nearly true notwithstanding any contrary hypotheses, until yet other phenomena make such propositions either more exact or liable to exceptions.[68]

Newton's method of demonstratively deriving laws from effects and then refining them against further observations was a powerful tool, in that it allowed for a wide-reaching empiricism which embraced 'all substances', including 'traditional metaphorical objects' like gravity that had been conventionally interpreted by means of conjectures

---

65   Newton, *Principia*, p. 793.
66   Newton, *Opticks*, pp. 404–405.
67   Newton, *Principia*, p. 795.
68   Ibid.

due to their invisibility.[69] While indeed, as argued in Query 31 of the *Opticks*, the causes of 'active principles' such as gravity cannot be discovered because they leave 'no impression on the senses', according to Newton we may still consider these principles 'not as occult qualities [...] but as general Laws of Nature, by which the Things themselves are form'd', and the reason is that their effects may be calculated mathematically, as long as one refrains from speculatively imagining their causes. Their truth, the excerpt continues, 'appears to us by Phaenomena', by which Newton means the reliable numerical data on which general laws are obtained.[70]

The ramifications of this insistence on phenomena as objective entities independent from any human explanatory effort can hardly be overestimated. It amounted, as Hylarie Kochiras argues, to the very core of Newton's intellectual legacy.[71] As a result of the diffusion of Newton's *hypotheses non fingo* methodology, British contemporaries felt, in Gerd Buchdahl's words, a 'new sense of power over nature' because they felt they could bestow 'the certainty of mathematics upon man's knowledge of physical phenomena'.[72]

Via popularisations and commentaries on Newton and his ideas, the complexity of *Principia* and *Opticks* was distilled into the perception that not only nature, but also moral phenomena could be finally discovered with certainty, regardless of whether Newton actually endorsed this position and without any clarity as to how this goal could be reached.[73] Crucially to the argument of this book, the fact that this Newtonianist sense of confidence was interlocked with a rejection of imagination-based hypotheses informed debates about the limits of the imagination. To be like Newton, observers were supposed to avoid over-relying on their imagination – that is, feigning hypotheses – because it adulterated

---

69   Hylarie Kochiras, 'Gravity and Newton's Substance Counting Problem', *Studies in History and Philosophy of Science*, 40 (2009), 267–280 (p. 270).

70   Newton, *Opticks*, p. 401.

71   Kochiras, p. 270.

72   Gerd Buchdahl, *The Image of Newton and Locke in the Age of Reason* (London and New York: Sheed and Ward, 1961), p. 5.

73   Following eighteenth-century usage, 'moral' (in expressions like 'moral philosophy' or 'moral science') is used for everything pertaining the study of humankind.

observations, failing to let nature speak in her own voice. In other words, Newtonianism promised certainty in knowledge-making enquiries, but this required the faculty of the imagination to be disciplined. Was it possible for people other than Newton to do so, and what did these limits to the imagination entail? To the influence of these two questions beyond natural philosophy, the next chapter now turns.

CHAPTER 2
BEYOND NATURAL PHILOSOPHY
The Confidence and Anxiety of Newtonianism

2.1. *Reason and the Ideal Newtonianist Subject*

Eighteenth-century poetry, drama and prose were replete with references to Newton. In many cases, this occurred because it was *à la mode* to do so. Writers felt compelled to mention Newton's name and discoveries to meet the expectations of their readers, so references were often trivial. In a poem by John Reynolds, an early eighteenth century poetaster, the 'Law of Love' is claimed to have been found thanks to a groundbreaking application of 'Newtonian Philosophy'.[1] In James Miller's play *The Humours of Oxford* (1730), beaux are described as being 'encompass'd with Telescopes and Globes, instead of Looking Glasses, and Peruke-Blocks', and coquettes as having 'Euclid and Newton on [their] Toilet, instead of Waller and Congreve'.[2] Newton's discoveries were represented as children's toys, as in John Newbery's *Philosophy of Tops and Balls* (1761), and Newton himself was likened to a late eighteenth-century wonder like the hot-air balloon, in that both soar to the sky leaving 'the stupid multitude below', as one learns from a poem by Mary Alcock.[3]

Instances like these serve to indicate not only that Newton's ideas were far-reaching, but also that they could influence the eighteenth-

---

1   John Reynolds, *Death's Vision Represented in a Philosophical, Sacred Poem* (London: T. Parkhust, 1709), p. 8.
2   Quoted in Chico, p. 55.
3   John Newbery, *The Newtonian System of Philosophy. Adapted to the Capacities of Young Gentlemen and Ladies, and familiarized and made entertaining by Objects with which they are intimately acquainted* (London: John Newbery, 1761), p. 22; Mary Alcock, *The Air Balloon: Or, Flying Mortal. A Poem* (London: E. Macklew, 1784), p. 4.

century literary imagination in a rather loose manner. As a whole, the body of Newton-related references one finds in the literary works published at this time takes the shape of a kaleidoscope of textual fragments, some of which germane to Newton's original ideas, but many less so; some consciously used to advance specific agendas, but others just occasional references with no specific purpose other than the very act of naming Newton.

However, there were also literary works that elaborated on the confidence in human knowledge-making abilities which characterised Newtonianism, and especially on the key question of the scope that was to be given to the imagination. With his methodology, Newton had recast the all-too-human inclination to come up with imaginative explanations as a disruptive factor which adulterates observations of nature. Earlier natural philosophers had taken advantage of varying degrees of subjective interpretation to make sense of phenomena they could not verify by observation, but Newton believed that doing so was the equivalent of coming up with fictional explanations. It was not enough for a given hypothesis to be verisimilar, for only when a phenomenon is fully ascertained can a statement be made about the way nature works. Nor was probability sufficient, for, in Newton's own premonitory words from the *Optical Lectures* he delivered in Cambridge between 1670 and 1672, the only way to 'finally achieve a natural science supported by the greatest evidence' is with the 'help of philosophical geometers and geometrical philosophers, instead of the conjectures and probabilities that are being blazoned about everywhere'.[4]

The preface to the second edition of the *Principia*, written by Roger Cotes under Newton's close supervision, resorted to literary analogies to convey the condemnation of the imagination in the strongest manner. The 'true constitutions of things is obviously to be sought in vain from false conjectures', and persevering in this habit, as many do, is tantamount to 'drifting off into dreams', or, what is worse, writing a 'romance':

---

4   Isaac Newton, *The Optical Papers of Isaac Newton. Vol. 1, The Optical Lectures, 1670–1672*, ed. by Alan E. Shapiro (Cambridge: Cambridge University Press, 1984), pp. 88–89.

> Those who take the foundation of their speculations from hypotheses [...] even if they then proceed most rigorously according to mechanical laws, are merely putting together a romance, elegant perhaps and charming, but nevertheless a romance.[5]

It is only through an unadulterated observation of the 'true constitution of things' undisturbed by the human imagination that accurate knowledge is to be made. Doing otherwise is the same as writing romances – fantastical stories that, for all their beauty, have no connection to the nature of things. As it was put by John Theophilus Desaguliers in 1734, a public demonstrator who had also been close to Newton, hypotheses are the resource of people with 'warm Imaginations', and must be confuted by 'daily Observations and common Laws of Motion'.[6]

The indictment of the imagination advocated by Newton and his followers was an unrealistic knowledge-making standard that not even Newton himself was able to meet. In fact, evidence shows that Newton resorted to the faculty of the imagination on several occasions. To tackle the astronomical problems of the *Principia*, especially that of the force of gravity which is mutually exerted by celestial bodies, he had to create simplified imaginative scenarios which allowed him to focus on a limited number of factors.[7] Moreover, as some of his contemporaries were quick to point out, Newton *did* use conjectures in his scientific practice. The most glaring instance was the law of universal gravitation, whose causes Newton left undetermined to the bewilderment of philosophers like Leibniz, who retorted that to conceive of gravity in such a way was no different to making use of occult qualities.[8] Newton was aware of this issue, and he attempted

---

5   Roger Cotes, 'Editor's Preface to the Second Edition', in Isaac Newton, *Philosophiae Naturalis Principia Mathematica*, ed. by I. Bernard Cohen, trans. by Anne Whitman (Berkeley, Los Angeles, and London: University of California Press, 1999), pp. 385–399 (p. 386).

6   John Theophilus Desaguliers, *A Course of Experimental Philosophy* (London: John Senex, 1734), 'Preface'. On Desaguliers, see Audrey T. Carpenter, *John Theophilus Desaguliers: A Natural Philosopher, Engineer and Freemason in Newtonian England* (London and New York: Continuum, 2011).

7   See Cohen, *Newtonian Revolution*, pp. 52–154.

8   Ori Belkind, 'Leibniz and Newton on Space', *Foundations of Science*, 18 (2013), 467–497 (p. 470). These contradictions in Newton's thought led

several times to come up with a hypothesis to explain how the force of gravity really worked. The most famous case is Query 29 of the *Opticks*, which cautiously postulates the presence of an invisible aether standing in-between all celestial bodies and conveying the force of gravity through mechanical means.[9]

That explains why George Gordon, one of the few British natural philosophers who remained unimpressed by Newton's achievements, remarked that Newton's 'Motions of the Heavens' were as 'many Instances of unintelligible Causes'. Evoking a power of attraction universal to all bodies was in open contrast with the *hypotheses non fingo* approach, so, drawing on a literary metaphor himself, Gordon concluded that Newton's argument for an invisible, unverified power of attraction looked just 'as monstrous as any of the Fictions of Antiquity; and the Mathematical Dress of the Arguments which support that Cause, does not hinder me from suspecting their Sufficiency'.[10]

Such criticism shows that Newton's stated methodology on banishing hypotheses to achieve mathematical certainty was one based on an idealized human observer rather than an empirical one. However, notwithstanding Newton's own inconsistencies in the use of hypotheses, his commentators created an image of him which embodied the unattainable ideal subject that the Newtonianist methodology seemed to demand – i.e., an observer whose study

---

historian of science Valerio Ronchi to argue that that of Newton is 'an incoherent and uncertain theory, a theory so full of contradictions and lacunae that one is surprised to see to what extent it could convince the majority of the physicists of the 18th century'. In Paul Feyerabend, 'Classical Empiricism', *The Methodological Heritage of Newton*, ed. by Robert E. Butts and John W. Davis (Toronto: University of Toronto Press, 1970), pp. 150–170 (p. 164n11).

9   While Newton disclaimed that, since his conjecture was in the Queries (which he meant as a section created on purpose to entertain hypotheses) it had nothing to do with the establishment of matter of fact, he was privately convinced that it was 'inconceivable, that inanimate brute Matter should, without the Mediation of something else, which is not material, operate upon, and affect other Matter without mutual Contact'. This he stated in his third letter to Richard Bentley, the first Boyle Lecturer in 1692. In Isaac Newton, *Four Letters from Sir Isaac Newton to Doctor Bentley, Containing Some Arguments in Proof of a Deity* (London: R. and J. Dodsley, 1756), p. 25.

10   George Gordon, *Remarks Upon the Newtonian Philosophy* (London: J. Peele, 1719), p. 6.

of natural phenomena was imagination-free. It was an image that lasted for the whole eighteenth century, so much so that in 1774 an anonymous journalist of the *London Chronicler* could still praise Newton for having 'such a mastery over his imagination'.[11] The famous historian of science Alexandre Koyré once wrote that Newton's legacy lies precisely in the abolishment of the 'world of qualities and sense perception, the world of appreciation of our daily life', replacing it with a 'universe of precision, of exact measures, of strict determination'.[12] Much more so than any specific discoveries in astronomy or optics, it was this ideal of the Newtonian observer of nature, embodied by a mythologized image of Newton himself, which proved influential in the culture of eighteenth-century Britain.

The faculty of reason was what encoded the ideal Newtonianist subject's ability to eschew conjectures. In *A View of Sir Isaac Newton's Philosophy*, Pemberton describes Newton as a turning point in history because he had done 'honour to human nature, by having extended the greatest and most noble of our faculties, reason, to subjects, which, till he attempted them, appeared to be wholly beyond of our limited capacities'.[13] He was not alone in this assessment. As Voltaire reports in his *Philosophical Letters*, Newton was characterized by the faculty of reason to such a degree that he had been able to illuminate the secrets of nature. Because of this, Voltaire adds, British people were persuaded that no less than 'a new Universe' had been discovered.[14]

Historically, reason had long tended to be understood as a faculty that, while conducive to discoveries about nature, had limited powers because of its subordination to faith. One of the most prominent commentators who endorsed this view was theologian Richard Hooker, especially with his influential *Of the Laws of Ecclesiastical Polity* (first published in 1594, but often reprinted in the seventeenth and eighteenth century). According to Hooker,

---

11   *London Chronicle or Universal Evening Post* (London, England), November 12, 1774 – November 15, 1774; Issue 2798.

12   Alexandre Koyré, *Newtonian Studies* (London: Chapman and Hall, 1965), p. 5.

13   Pemberton, 'Dedication'.

14   Voltaire, Letters, p. 122.

reason is 'the director of man's will by discovering in action what is good'. The very 'laws of well-doing', Hooker explains, 'are the dictates of right reason', whereas, when reason errs, 'we fall into evil'.[15] The currency of these views in the late seventeenth century is testified by John Dryden's poem *Religio Laici; or a Layman's Faith* (1682), a work which places itself in continuity with Hooker's position by underlining reason's meagre explanatory power when compared to faith. Reason's 'glimmering light', Dryden writes, pales 'at religion's sight', and is eventually dissolved by the 'supernatural light' of God. Even more so than Hooker, who is optimistic about the reliability of reason in everyday matters, Dryden conceives of reason and faith as two separate, non-reconcilable types of light, with the latter enjoying an indisputable superiority over the former.[16]

This should not be taken to imply that 'reason' was not praised as crucial to early science prior to Newton. For instance, in his ode titled 'To the Royal Society', which prefaced Thomas Sprat's *History of the Royal Society* (1667), Abraham Cowley describes Lord Bacon as the one who chased away idolatrous belief in past authorities with 'the plain magic of true reason's light'.[17] But doing so was not without risks of criticism. In fact, Dryden's insistence on the hierarchical superiority of faith to reason in *Religio Laici* was partly a reaction to the rise of experimental philosophy in England, which many feared would displace providence as the primary explanatory framework for natural knowledge.[18]

As shown by Pemberton's confidence that reason was the most important faculty that man could aspire to, however, it is evident

---

15   Richard Hooker, *Of the Laws of Ecclesiastical Polity*, ed. by Arthur Stephen McGrade (Cambridge: Cambridge University Press, 2002), pp. 72, 75.

16   John Dryden, *The Works of John Dryden*, ed. by H.T. Swedenberg and Edward Niles Hooker (Oxford: Oxford University Press, 1956), II, 242. On Dryden's religious allegiances, see Douglas G. Atkins, *The Faith of John Dryden: Change and Continuity* (Lexington: University Press of Kentucky, 1980); John West, *Dryden and Enthusiasm: Literature, Religion and Politics in Restoration England* (Oxford: Oxford University Press, 2018).

17   In Thomas Sprat, *The history of the Royal-Society of London for the improving of natural knowledge* (London: J. Martyn and J. Allestry, 1667), 'To The Royal Society'.

18   Thomas H. Fujimura, 'Dryden's *Religio Laici*: An Anglican Poem', *PMLA*, 76 (1961), 205–217 (pp. 206–207).

that a shift had taken place by the turn of the century. Samuel Clarke, one of Newton's disciples in his later years, preached in one of his 1705 Boyle Lectures that the 'constant and sincere observance of all the Laws of Reason and Obligations to Natural Religion, will unavoidably lead a Man to Christianity'.[19] Reason is praised unconditionally by Clarke, with no suggestion that it clashes with faith; on the contrary, what is stressed is its being the ability allowing man to clearly see through nature and, thanks to that, understand God's design.[20]

Once the Newtonian light of reason started being praised by his contemporaries, commentators were faced with the problem of whether this quality was one that anyone could develop, or whether Newton had been exceptional and, thus, beyond comparison. These two claims could find some common ground in the image of Newton as a benevolent demi-God who, like a novel Prometheus, had gifted humanity with the light of reason. Partisan commentators like Halley and Pemberton persistently conveyed an image of Newton which synthesised intellectual exceptionality and public generosity. In particular, Halley's ode depicted Newton as the man who had been blessed by the divinities with the ability to unlock 'the treasure chest of Hidden Truth', but who then extended this remarkable gift to the rest of humankind. 'Mortals', Halley wrote, can 'arise' and 'put aside earthly cares, / And from this treatise [the *Principia*] discern the power of a mind sprung from heaven'.[21]

Newton, the argument went, had unveiled the secrets of nature and shown them to everybody, in effect putting within reach knowledge which had been thought to be beyond the human intellect. This increasingly common position was also voiced by Voltaire, who in his *The Elements of Sir Isaac Newton's Philosophy* (originally published in France in 1737 and translated into English in the same year) argued that Newton's ideas are directed towards 'the Improvement of all such as desire to cultivate their Reason', so

---

19   In Stewart, p. 75.

20   John Gascoigne, *Joseph Banks and the English Enlightenment: Useful Knowledge and Polite Culture* (Cambridge and New York: Cambridge University Press, 1994), p. 32.

21   In Newton, *Principia*, pp. 379–380.

that everybody is able 'to conceive certain Truths aright'. Newton is portrayed by Voltaire as the exemplary man who had simplified the complexity of nature, making it understandable to everybody: 'The Knowledge of Nature is a Good, to which all Men have an equal Right: all are for knowing their Good, which few have Time or Patience to calculate; this *Newton* has done for them'.[22] Accordingly, a number of eighteenth-century poets readily correlated Newton's reason to a shining light illuminating fellow philosophers as well as lay-people. As Nicolson showed, eighteenth-century poets 'adored the greater luminary, symbol of Light, symbol of Reason', the 'Newtonian Sun'.[23] The likes of James Thomson, Mark Akenside and Edward Young often associated Newton with light. As Thomson once put it, Newton was 'our philosophic sun' – as the latter conveys warmth to people, so Newton transmitted his reason to fellow citizens.[24]

In other cases, however, there was some lurking scepticism as to whether anyone could be endowed with the gift of a Newton-like reason. This problem is posed, for instance, by Fontenelle in his *Éloge de Isaac Newton*, a work based on the notes collected by John Conduitt and translated into English in 1728. Fontenelle makes the point that '[w]hen we are for prying into Nature, we ought to examine her like Sir Isaac—that is, in as accurate and importunate a manner'. Even that, however, might not be sufficient, for some phenomena escape observation, 'almost hid[ing] themselves from our enquiries, as being of too abstracted a nature'. These evasive phenomena Newton knew 'how to reduce to calculation', but 'such calculations might elude the Skill of the best Geometricians, without that Dexterity which was peculiar to himself'.[25]

As Fontenelle elevates Newton as the best possible observer of nature, he implicitly poses the question of whether his reason could be employed by anybody other than him. Nonetheless, this

---

22   François-Marie Arouet de Voltaire, *The Elements of Sir Isaac Newton's Philosophy. Translated from the French* (London: Stephen Austen, 1737), pp. 1–4.

23   Nicolson, p. 32.

24   In Nicolson, p. 43. On Thomson's Newtonianism, see Fairer, pp. 285–286.

25   Bernard Le Bovier de Fontenelle, *An Account of the Life and Writings of Sir Isaac Newton* (London: James Woodman and David Lyon, 1728), p. 21.

acknowledgment of the gap between the capabilities of Newton and those of other people did not necessarily result in a negative outlook. Fontenelle eventually suggests that a change might be underway, the deficiencies of humankind being progressively mitigated by the development of Newtonian 'reason'.[26]

Other commentators were more prudent. Pemberton recognized that Newton's 'reason' might after all be difficult to attain for others because the rigidity of Newton's own method, which required something of a super-human objectivity, was at odds with the actual limited capabilities of man. The 'reason' which Newton had made available to the many was 'that faculty, whereon the conduct of our lives, and our happiness depends'. And yet, the complete interdiction of hypotheses was a very restrictive requirement that only Newton could meet.[27] This is why Pemberton makes allowances for the limited capacities of humankind by astutely reframing the method of Newton as an ideal to aspire to, rather than a goal that could be realistically attained:

> The proof in natural philosophy cannot be so absolutely conclusive, as in mathematics. For the subjects of that science are purely the ideas of our own minds. [...] But in natural knowledge the subject of our contemplation is without us, and not so compleatly to be known: therefore our method of arguing must fall a little short of perfection.[28]

Even if Newton's 'reason' does not readily belong to ordinary people because their abilities fall 'a little short of perfection', Pemberton identifies a 'just course' between 'the conjectural method of proceeding' and 'demanding so rigorous a proof, as will reduce all philosophy to mere scepticism, and exclude all prospect of making any progress in the knowledge of nature'.[29]

---

26 Fontenelle's celebration of Newton was interlaced with the dispute between ancient and moderns which animated the first decades of the eighteenth century. For an overview, see Joseph M. Levine, *The Battle of the Books: History and Literature in the Augustan Age* (Cornell: Cornell University Press, 1991), chapter one.
27 Pemberton, 'Dedication'.
28 Pemberton, p. 23.
29 Ibid.

With the intent of brokering a mediation between the lofty example of Newton as an enlightened observer of nature and the more modest human capabilities of everyone else, Pemberton proceeds to argue that the characteristic common to both Newton and lay people is a natural inclination to search for truth. Nothing is more suitable to the human mind, Pemberton writes, than 'the contemplation of truth', and 'all men are moved with a strong desire after knowledge, esteeming it honourable to excel therein; and holding it, on the contrary, disgraceful to mistake, err, or be in any way deceived'.[30] This is a way for Pemberton to reduce the importance given to the faculty of the imagination while acknowledging the inevitability of recurring to it. In a complex balancing act, Pemberton's reading repurposes Newton's *hypotheses non fingo*, making it less a strict prohibition than a strong declaration of intent. Like Newton, every person who aims to understand the workings of nature must feel unsatisfied with knowledge obtained by recourse to hypotheses; they too, like the philosopher, must aim at the establishment of truth, even if it might be impossible for them to do so with absolute certainty because the faculty of imagination cannot be fully done without.

2.2. *The Diminishing Role of Humankind*

Complex discursive renderings of Newton's methodology such as Pemberton's worked to preserve the confidence that a certainty like that claimed by Newton was within human reach despite the obvious limitations of man. Crucial to making sure Newton's reason was not perceived as an otherworldly ability were texts such as Francesco Algarotti's *Newtonianismo per le dame* (1736), which was promptly translated into English by Elizabeth Carter and enjoyed great popularity amongst polite London readers. Although originally produced for a different cultural context, Algarotti's work contributed to the British debate about Newtonianism by striking a balance between preserving the confidence in reason derived

------

30   Pemberton, p. 2.

from Newton and making it into a less exclusive quality. With the goal of allowing his public to feel empowered by Newton's reason without their having to master mathematics, Algarotti revisits Newton's ideas to make them more readily acceptable to his readers. His popularization is paradoxically 'a Work of Philosophy and Politeness' where the 'reason' granted by the use of Newton's method could be shared by virtually anybody, as long as they do not attempt to impose their ideas on other people:

> Let the Age of Realities once more arise among us, and Knowledge instead of giving a rude and savage Turn to the Mind, and exciting endless Disputes and wrangling upon some obsolete Phrase, serve to polish and adorn Society.[31]

Reason is converted by Algarotti into a blend of social appropriacy and Newtonianist confidence about knowledge-making. Following the polysemy of the Italian word *ragione*, Carter's translation of the beginning of the first dialogue keeps the narrator's pun that '[t]he very same Reason that led me every Day to a Concert of Music, a gay and elegant Entertainment, a Ball, or the Theatre induced me to write'.[32] Reason in this sense conjoins two apparently contradictory strands: the faculty of casting light on the deeper mystery of nature, and the ability to avoid disputes by discarding the assertiveness that was inherent in Newton's mathematics.

Others who endorsed the confidence in Newton's reason, however, were less prone to compromises. Some likened themselves to Newton in fields such as religion or moral philosophy, a claim that spurred serious questions about the diminishing role of humankind in a Newtonian universe. George Cheyne's *Philosophical Principles of Natural Religion* (1705) is a particularly salient example. In this work aimed at proving the existence of God, and whose title clearly echoes Newton's *Principia*, past authorities are excluded because deemed unreliable compared to what Cheyne calls 'demonstration'. In the preface to his work, Cheyne explains that he 'industriously avoided all Quotations, because [the] Subject wanted not *Authorities*;

---

31   Algarotti, pp. xi, xvi.
32   Algarotti, p. 1.

but *Demonstrations*'.[33] While past sources are eventually cited, it is significant that Cheyne feels compelled to ground his enquiry on the idea that authorities, no matter how prestigious or creditable, are no different to subjective opinions that must be discarded because adulterated by the imagination.

The systematic exclusion of authorities configures a universe in which man is a negligible presence in the face of nature. It is telling that Cheyne conceptualizes the universe as a 'vast, if not infinite *Machin* of the *Universe*, the Perfect and Wise Production of Almighty God consisting of an infinite number of lesser *Machines*, every one of which is adjusted by Weight and Measure'. As a mechanism set in motion by God, nature does not require the presence of man to function. From this conceptual standpoint, it is a short step to argue that nature, and the God that created it, are indifferent to the presence of human beings. Cheyne does not go as far as making this claim, but his insistence on a mechanical universe implies that the benchmark for accurate knowledge was not based on human abilities. The 'System of Universe', he contends, must be 'liken'd to a finish'd Piece of Clockwork form'd upon *Geometrick* Principles'. To determine the principles of religion with the certainty of demonstration, Cheyne goes as far as excluding living creatures, and his work is accordingly premised by the warning that he 'shall not here consider the Actions of Beings, that have a Power of *Free-Will*', because these would interfere with the establishment of knowledge on a demonstrative basis.[34]

Cheyne is one of the many who were exalted by the epistemic possibilities offered by Newton's ideas, and believed himself to be endowed with the same reason Newton had. Other commentators, however, were more perturbed by the question of whether humankind is equipped with 'reason' enough to make knowledge in Newtonianist terms. A significant example comes from a 1731 issue of the *Grub Street Journal*, which adversely reviewed Pemberton's *A View of Sir Isaac Newton's Philosophy* because of its emphasis on reason as a quality that yields indisputable truths. The epigraph chosen by the

---

33   George Cheyne, *Philosophical Principles of Natural Religion* (London: George Strahan, 1705), p. 2.
34   Cheyne, p. 5.

newspaper was, emblematically, a couplet from Dryden's *The Hind and the Panther* (1687), whose preparatory poem, the *Religio Laici*, chastised the emphasis on reason placed by early scientists in the late seventeenth century, as examined above. The lines chosen in *Grub Street Journal* are the famous couplet 'Let Reason then at her own quarry fly: / But how can finite grasp infinity?'.[35] To the *Grub Street Journal* writer, the question of reason was decisive: could a being as little equipped with reason as man really make sense of the divine universe which Newton had unveiled in the *Principia*?

The nature discovered by Newton, with its immutable, universal, and yet mysterious laws, entailed problematical conclusions about the knowledge-making powers of humankind. Joseph Addison's definition of Newton as 'the Miracle of the present Age' in a 1712 *The Spectator* issue was clearly celebrative, but its wording entails that Newton was by some perceived as an exceptional case in the history of humankind.[36] Not that normal people are unequipped with reason, Addison claims in the same piece, but their reason operates on a very different level from that of Newton in terms of what can be grasped intellectually. Newton's reason made him able to 'look through a whole Planetary System', whereas our understanding is 'more confined':

> The more extended our Reason is, and the more able to grapple with immense Objects, the greater still are those Discoveries which it makes of Wisdom and Providence in the Work of the Creation. A Sir *Isaac Newton*, who stands up as the Miracle of the Present Age, can look through a whole Planetary System; consider it in its Weight, Number, and Measure; and draw from it as many Demonstrations of infinite Power and Wisdom, as a more confined Understanding is able to deduce from the System of an Human Body.[37]

The fear that Newton had been extraordinary, and not merely exemplary, led to uneasy reflections about the actual abilities of the rest of humankind. William Warburton's 1740 influential commentary on Pope's *An Essay on Man* (1733) is one of the key texts to explore

---

35 *Grub Street Journal*, Thursday, May 20, 1731; Issue 72.
36 *The Spectator*, Saturday, November 22, 1712; Issue 543.
37 Ibid.

this anxiety. Warburton, who had been Pope's chosen editor of the *Dunciad*, reads *An Essay on Man* as a sustained discussion on the flawed conditions of human understanding. According to Warburton, Pope is not just the poet who keeps in check human ambition by restoring it to its rightful place within the great chain of beings, but a sceptical thinker who describes 'the dark and feeble State of the human Understanding' compared to the epistemic standard set by Newton.[38] This argument is specifically made with regard to the 'Knowledge of ourselves' – that is, the problem of whether laws as universal and immutable as those discovered by Newton could be found in the study of human nature too – a question to which Warburton responded in the negative, for it is a 'Fact' that the '*clearest* Science, which results from the *Newtonian* Philosophy' does not translate to the study of man.[39]

Pope's *An Essay on Man* was often the vehicle through which anxieties such as Warburton's were conveyed, possibly because of Pope's own ambiguities in committing to Newton's ideas.[40] In the close to epistle one, Pope warns philosophers not to presume they knew too much of nature, because they too were slaves to 'erring reason'.[41] In the second epistle, which starts with the famous couplet 'Know then thyself, presume not God to scan; / The proper study of mankind is man', Pope resumes his attack on overly-ambitious philosophers by satirically inviting one of them to:

> Go, wondrous creature! mount where science guides,
> Go, measure earth, weigh air, and state the tides;

---

38   William Warburton, *A Vindication of Mr. Pope's Essay on Man, from the Misrepresentations of Mr de Crousaz* (London: J. Robinson, 1740), p. 50. Warburton's commentary was published in reaction to the attack on the morality and theology of Pope's *Essay* by Jean Pierre de Crousaz, a Swiss mathematician. See Elise F. Knapp, 'Community Property: The Case for Warburton's 1751 Edition of Pope', *Studies in English Literature, 1500–1900*, 26 (1986), 455–468.

39   Ibid.

40   See B. W. Young, '"See Mystery to Mathematics Fly": Pope's *Dunciad* and the Critique of Religious Rationalism', *Eighteenth-Century Studies*, 26 (1993), 435–448.

41   Alexander Pope, *An Essay on Man*, ed. by Tom Jones (Princeton: Princeton University Press, 2016), Epistle I, ll. 293–294.

> Instruct the planets in what orbs to run,
> Correct old time, and regulate the sun. (Epistle II, ll. 19–22)

While this image most likely pieces together the achievements of different early scientists, the references to planetary orbits and ancient chronology show that Newton was unmistakably in Pope's mind. A few lines afterwards, however, Newton is mentioned as the man whom Gods show around in heaven 'as we shew an *Ape*' because of his exceptionality as the 'mortal Man' who 'unfold[ed] all Nature's law' (ll. 32, 34).

Charles A. Beaumont notes that Pope's 'does not oppose an intellectually gifted man who can soar as high as a comet, if such a man knows his place in God's order and is merely investigating the physical order', but some ambiguity on his position on Newton remains, as some of his eighteenth-century readers perceived.[42] Making once more use of Pope as a palimpsest, the front-page article of the *Universal Spectator and Weekly Journal* of 23 March 1745 reports that not even Newton, this 'great Philosopher', knew 'more of *himself* than another Mortal' because (with yet another reference to *An Essay on Man*) for him too '*Passion* [...] *undoes what Reason weaves*'.[43] If the genial Newton could not fully trust his reason, how could the rest of humankind hope to compare?

As David Hume had put it in the final appendix to the sixth volume of the *History of England* published in 1754, it might well be the case that Newton had only *seemed* to solve the mystery of nature to the benefit of everyone, only for time to reveal that his discoveries could not be partaken to by others. Newton, Hume suggests with careful verb choice, 'seemed to draw off the veil from some of the mysteries of nature', but, as he died, he eventually 'restored her ultimate secrets to that obscurity in which they ever did and ever will remain'.[44] Concluding his historical narrative with the future

---

42   Charles A. Beaumont, 'The Rising and Falling Metaphor in Pope's 'An Essay on Man', *Style*, 1 (1967), 121–130 (p. 124).

43   *Universal Spectator and Weekly Journal*, Saturday, March 23, 1745; Issue 859.

44   David Hume, *The History of England from the Invasion of Julius Caesar to the Revolution in 1688*, 6 vols, ed. by William B. Todd (Indianapolis: Liberty Fund, 1983), VI, 542.

tense, Hume recognizes Newton's genius, but predicts that, exactly because of this, nature will forever be unknowable because Newton's own exceptionality, which could not be replicated, had the function of shedding light on the knowledge-making shortcomings of man.

This evidence serves to show that the Newtonianist intellectual climate was a mixed one where confidence in human knowledge-making abilities was blended with anxiety about human shortcomings. The image of Newton, with its emphasis on his extraordinary, super-human reason, paradoxically resulted in distrust of one's own understanding. It was once again Addison who most eloquently voiced this anxiety, no doubt because it must have engrossed the thoughts of the reading public of *The Spectator*, an outlet which had been regularly used by Addison to promote interest in natural philosophy.[45] In a narrative piece published in July 1714, Mr. Spectator reflects on the possibility that the advent of Newton deprived humankind of their ability to make sense of nature. Telling the story of a walk at dusk, he lifts his eyes to the skies and gazes at 'the Richness and Variety of Colours, which appeared in the Western Parts of Heaven: In Proportion as they faded away and went out, several Stars and Planets appeared one after another 'till the whole Firmament was in a Glow'.[46]

Such a beginning seems an instance of what Sarah Tindal Kareem called the layman's changed relationship 'to the cosmos', which thanks to Newton had shifted from 'primitive awe' to 'admiration for its newly explicable aesthetic spectacle'.[47] Indirectly referencing Newton, Addison writes of 'the *Æther*' of the '*Galaxy*' that 'appeared in its most beautiful White' and, to 'compleat the Scene', he looks at the beautiful 'full Moon'. The universe Addison beholds is that discovered by Newton, but admiration soon gives way to concern. Falling into a contemplative mood, he addresses God pathetically: '[w]hen I consider the Heavens the Work of thy Fingers, the Moon and the Stars which thou hast ordained; what is man that thou art mindful of him, and the son of man that thou regardest him!'. The

---

45   Lynall, p. 10.
46   *The Spectator*, Friday, July 9, 1714; Issue 565.
47   Sarah Tindal Kareem, *Eighteenth-Century Fiction and the Reinvention of Wonder* (Oxford: Oxford University Press, 2014), p. 132.

sight of 'that infinite Host of Stars, or, to speak more Philosophically, of Suns, which were then shining upon me, with those innumerable Sets of Planets or Worlds, which were moving round their respective Suns' prompts him to consider his place in the universe that Newton had unveiled:

> When I still enlarged the Idea, and supposed another Heaven of Suns and Worlds rising still above this which we discovered, and these still enlightened by a superior Firmament of Luminaries, which are planted at so great a Distance, that they may appear to the Inhabitants of the former as the Stars do to us; In short, whilst I pursued this Thought, I could not but reflect on that little insignificant Figure which I my self bore amidst the Immensity of God's Works.[48]

This fear of insignificance promptly leads to the contemplation of an apocalyptic scenario where the solar system to which our planet belongs is obliterated. 'Were the Sun, which enlightens this Part of the Creation, with all the Host of Planetary Worlds, that move about him, utterly extinguished and annihilated', Addison reflects, they would 'not be missed more than a grain of Sand upon the Sea-shore'. Developing this image of an infinite universe in which our planet is but a tiny speck, Addison's description escalates into a large-scale representation of the universe as an entity which cannot be apprehended by the human senses. Were our solar system to disappear, its absence would be 'scarce a *Blank* in the Creation', one imperceptible 'to an Eye, that could take in the whole Compass of Nature, and pass from one end of the Creation to the other'.[49]

Even after conceding that 'the Universe has certain Bounds set to it', Addison is worried that the human imagination is simply unable to grasp the immensity of the cosmos. When we consider that the universe is 'the Work of infinite Power, prompted by infinite Goodness, with an infinite Space to exert it self in, how can our Imagination set any Bounds to it?'[50] Human powerlessness, Addison

---

48   Ibid.
49   Ibid.
50   Ibid.

suggests, is nowhere more apparent than in our inability to grasp the immensity of the universe Newton had discovered.

2.3. *Religion and the Fear of a Mechanical Universe*

Contributions like Addison's reveal that the confidence in certainty promoted by the commentaries on Newton could also trigger the challenging realization that humankind was a negligible part of an enormous universe. God, which, Addison claims, created the universe thanks to 'infinite Power' and 'prompted by infinite Goodness', traditionally acted as the intermediary allowing man to understand natural phenomena within a providential framework. But why should humankind be a concern for God in such a vast universe? This question troubles Addison, who in the *Spectator* piece discussed above comes to the frightful realization that, in the universe discovered by Newton, humankind is of such little importance that we might well be disregarded by God. With 'secret Horrour', Addison is forced to contemplate the possibility that he was a being:

> not worth the smallest Regard of one who had so great a Work under his Care and Superintendency. I was afraid of being overlooked amidst the Immensity of Nature, and lost among that infinite Variety of Creatures, which in all Probability swarm through all these immeasurable Regions of Matter.[51]

Addison's *Spectator* piece ends on a positive note by considering that such a 'mortifying thought' is due to our 'narrow conceptions' of God. This common appeal for man not to pretend to know too much, however, is made via an admission of human shortcomings – the fact that '[w]e ourselves cannot attend to many different objects at the same time' – which is at odds with the ability of a Newton to unveil the secrets of nature. Raising the possibility that human reason was bound to be ineffective because prejudices are 'natural to the Mind of Man', Addison intimates that it was not possible

---

51   Ibid.

for man to follow in Newton's steps, nature being far beyond our knowledge-making capabilities.[52]

In other words, falling back to revelation to make sense of the unexplained had become more difficult after Newton. In the third volume of his *Moral Philosopher* (1740), Thomas Morgan expaxiates on the very question of how Newtonianism had affected the importance of religion as a framework of interpretation for natural phenomena. Building on the common use of the religious word 'Revelation', Morgan explains that the standard for making knowledge in both natural and moral phenomena had changed, for all knowledge must now have its foundation 'in Nature and Reason':

> [I]t is the Authority and Manner of Conveyance and Teaching, that gives it the Name of *Revelation*, but its necessary Foundation in Nature and Reason makes it a *true Doctrine*, and the Authority or Manner of Conveyance cannot alter, or affect this. Nothing that is antecedently and necessarily true in Nature and Reason, can depend on Authority for the Truth of it, since the very Authority itself must depend on the same Nature and Reason of Things. The same Truths or Doctrines may be receiv'd and adher'd to, either upon original, native Evidence, as founded in Nature and Reason, or by Authority from others, without any other Reason or Ground of Truth to those who thus take them upon Trust.[53]

Morgan's contrast between religious 'Revelation' and the 'Nature and Reason of Things' brings to the fore the problem of God's active intervention in natural phenomena. As Jacob has reconstructed, early Newtonians had claimed that God could intervene at any time on its creation, suspending its own rules as necessary. Even gravity, whose workings remained unclear, could always be explained by saying that it was an effect of divine intervention, i.e., God's continuous miracle to overcome the unexplained lack of mechanical contact between bodies.[54]

---

52 Ibid.

53 Morgan, III, 126.

54 Margaret C. Jacob, 'Newtonian Science and the Radical Enlightenment', *Vistas in Astronomy*, 22 (1979), 545–555 (p. 547).

There were groups of people, such as the High-Church Anglicans, who objected on the grounds that this position downplayed revelation.[55] In particular, the theological dispute between Leibniz and Clarke mentioned earlier in this chapter produced uneasiness because it prefigured the possibility that in a universe with immutable laws of nature, God does not need to intervene at all. In the metaphor proposed by John Gascoigne, the Leibniz controversy represents the realization that a universe based on Newton's ideas was one caught between 'the Scylla of continual divine intervention and the Charybdis of a form of naturalism which minimized God's activity'. These two alternatives were eloquently expressed by Leibniz himself:

> If God is oblig'd to mend the course of nature from time to time, it must be done either supernaturally or naturally. If it be done supernaturally, we must have recourse to miracles, in order to explain natural things: which is reducing an hypothesis ad absurdum: for, every thing may easily be accounted for by miracles. But if it be done naturally, then God will not be *intelligentia supramundane*; he will be comprehended under the nature of things; that is, he will be the soul of the world.[56]

In other words, if one accepted the argument made by Newton and his commentators that nature is regulated by a finite set of immutable and universally valid laws, then there was little need for God to intervene in the vicissitudes of humankind via acts of providence. The very concept of a watchmaker God endorsed by the early Newtonians entails that, while God could potentially intervene at any moment, his only demonstrable intervention was the creation of the universe, which was then left to run by the perfect laws of nature discovered by Newton. Such a scenario makes 'revelation' superfluous, for natural phenomena occur because of the way nature was created by God to begin with.

An important aspect of the confidence associated with Newtonianism lies precisely in the fact that the advocates of the argument by design found that the reason-driven detection

---

55   Twombly, p. 255.
56   In Gascoigne, 'From Bentley', p. 227.

of regularity in natural phenomena could potentially replace 'supernatural' explanations, thus making revelation a redundant knowledge-making tool.[57] A few years after Clarke's dispute with Leibniz, William Whiston, another prominent early Newtonian, conceded that, when analysed through reason, everything that seems to be caused by the 'Power of Providence of God' is actually 'no more miraculous' than any other natural phenomenon:

> For those Events or Actions are in Holy Scripture attributed immediately to the Power of Providence of God, which yet were to all outward appearance according to the constant course of things, and would, abstracted from such Affirmation of the Holy Books, have been esteem'd no more miraculous than the other common Effects of Nature, or usual Accidents of Humane Affairs.[58]

With nature conceived in terms of laws that operate with perfect regularity, there is no need for miraculous interventions.[59] Therefore, human knowledge could technically consist only of the detection of what Pemberton calls the 'Universal properties' of nature through the use of 'reason', rather than of the interpretation of divine signs.[60]

This explains why many throughout the century would raise the spectre of divine revelation being superseded by natural philosophy. In an article in the *Whitehall Evening Post* of 12 April 1750, the anonymous author rails against the 'Naturalists', who, due to their 'little Smattering of the Theory concerning the Motion and Gravitation of Bodies', tend to be increasingly fixated on 'experiments in Natural Philosophy'. These Newtonian discoveries result in a 'little and imperfect Knowledge of the Works, and a much less one of the Author, of Nature'. It is all too easily forgotten that it was God who 'pleased to impress' on the universe its structure, so that 'certain Effects regularly follow certain Motions and Properties

---

57   See Peter Harrison, 'Newtonian Science, Miracles, and the Laws of Nature', *Journal of the History of Ideas*, 56 (1995), 531–553 (p. 541).

58   William Whiston, *New Theory of the Earth* (London: Benj. Tooke, 1696), p. 218f. On Whiston's allegiance to Newton's ideas and his complex religious outlook, see Force, *William Whiston*, pp. 121–155.

59   Buchdahl, pp. 9–10.

60   Pemberton, pp. 24–25.

of Matter, according to particular Laws'. By contrast, the naturalists claim that they 'can account for the motions and properties of matter 'from the Laws of Nature', and by doing so they, 'conscious of their immoral lives', 'deny the Operations of Providence' and 'shut God out of the World'.[61] The overt reference made by the writer to Pope's satirical lines in the *Dunciad* – 'And Philosophy, which lean'd on Heav'n before, / Shrinks to her Second Cause, and is no more' – are employed to express, and question, the Newtonianist shift which led to 'heaven' being less important than 'second causes'.[62] In the same *Whitehall Evening Post* article, Pope is once more appropriated, though this time with the lines of the *Essay on Man* on the destructive chaos of a universe ensuing from the Lucifer-like ambition of some people to climb higher in the ladder of knowledge.[63] Pope's lines are here used to offer an arresting depiction of a cosmos in which miraculous providence does not intervene to provide balance for the universe:

> Let earth unbalanc'd from her orbit fly,
> Planets and suns run lawless through the sky;
> Let ruling angels from their spheres be hurl'd,
> Being on being wreck'd, and world on world;
> Heav'n's whole foundations to their centre nod,
> And nature tremble to the throne of God.[64]

If the principle of God's constant intervention is withdrawn, the *Whitehall Evening Post* writer comments, 'the Universe would again become a Chaos'. Of course, this was a speculative provocation. Pope's lines are employed to advance the conclusion that, 'its Author, the God of Nature, is always, and every where', and that the motion of Bodies 'cannot otherwise happen' with 'the present Laws

---

61   *Whitehall Evening Post or London Intelligencer*, April 12, 1750 – April 14, 1750; Issue 651.

62   Alexander Pope, *The Dunciad in Four Books* (London, 1743), vv. 644–645.

63   On Pope's relevance to social and cultural events in eighteenth-century England, see Flavio Gregori, 'Introduction: Pope on the Margins and in the Center', *Studies in the Literary Imagination*, 38 (2005), i–xliv.

64   Pope, *An Essay on Man*, Epistle I, vv. 251–256.

of Nature [...] without a Miracle'.[65] Still, entertaining the possibility that nature's laws be suspended is the index of a deeply-rooted ambivalence on God's active presence in the universe, as testified by Pope's own proposed epitaph upon the death of Newton in 1727. With its oblique formulation, the couplet 'Nature and Nature's Laws lay hid in Night / God said, *Let Newton be*! and All was *Light*' highlights both that the universal principles of nature discovered by Newton prove the existence of a benevolent God interested in humankind *and* that in Newton's model of the universe God was not an indispensable presence.[66] Read in one sense, Newton's birth, and thus his discoveries, are divinely ordained (it is 'God' that says 'Let Newton be'). Read in another sense, however, what gets discovered is not God and his creation but 'Nature and Nature's Laws', almost as if divine intervention was limited to that single, exceptional spark and, afterwards, man was left to deal with an automated nature.[67]

This situation of heightened epistemic relevance of nature at the expense of religion was further dramatized by Edward Young in *A Night Address to the Deity* (1745). In Young's nightmarish vision, matter is portrayed as a self-sufficient entity that has qualities such as 'Thought', 'Judgment' and 'Genius' which traditionally had been the domain of humankind. In this extreme picture, God is not involved in revising the mechanisms of the universe because matter has its own free will and decides for itself. The result is a dramatic shift of attention from man to nature. Each 'sage Atom' mockingly reveals that a lump of earth is by far more important than a human being:

> Has Matter *more* than Motion? Has it Thought,
> Judgment, and Genius? Is it deeply learn'd
> In *Mathematics*? Has it fram'd *such* Laws,

---

65   *Whitehall Evening Post or London Intelligencer*, April 12, 1750 – April 14, 1750; Issue 651.

66   Alexander Pope, *Poetry of Alexander Pope*, ed. by John Butt (New Haven: Yale University Press, 1963), p. 808.

67   The latter view is examined in Gascoigne, 'From Bentley', p. 229. For a study that examines Pope's adherence to a Newton-inspired natural theology, see Claude Willan, 'The Proper Study of Mankind in Pope and Thomson', *ELH*, 84 (2017), 63–90.

> Which, but to *guess*, a Newton made immortal?—
> If so, how each *sage* Atom laughs at *me*,
> Who think a *Clod* inferior to a *Man*?[68]

Young conceptualises the heightened importance of nature to the absurd point that an atom may mock man for his inferiority in terms of importance in the universe. This satirical reversal of the natural order serves to remind Young's readers that in the universe discovered by Newton man has a very limited role compared to nature. At the same time, Young seems to suggest, there is little hope of acquiring Newton-like knowledge for, as the poet specifies with careful use of adjectives, Newton is 'immortal', therefore different from everybody else.[69]

2.4. *Towards Prose Narrative: Articulating the Limits of the Imagination*

The Newtonianist confidence and anxiety examined in the previous sections reverberated in debates about the nature of fiction and the role of the imagination in poetry produced in Britain throughout the eighteenth century. After Nicolson's famous argument on the aesthetic influence of Newton's *Opticks* on eighteenth-century poetry, commentators have identified various instances of reflections on the nature of poetical imagination related, directly or indirectly, to Newtonianist ideas. William Powell Jones argued that 'the old idea of harmony and order in the universe was given a new impetus by Newton's mathematical demonstrations in the *Principia*', especially

---

68   Edward Young, *The Consolation. Containing, Among Other Things, I. A Moral Survey of the Nocturnal Heavens. II. A Night-Address to the Deity* (London: G. Hawkins, 1745), p. 74.

69   Young's Newtonianism has often been taken for granted, as instanced by Robert J. Mayhew, *Landscape, Literature and English Religious Culture, 1660–1800: Samuel Johnson and Languages of Natural Description* (New York: Palgrave, 2004), p. 95. An examination of Young's scepticisms about the ramifications of Newton's natural philosophy is offered in Wayne C. Ripley, '"An Age More Curious, Than Devout": The Counter-Enlightenment Edward Young', *Eighteenth-Century Studies*, 49 (2016), 507–529.

in the cosmological poetry of Richard Blackmore, Henry Brooke, Moses Browne and Henry Baker.[70] More broadly, the leading lights of Augustan poetry were highly receptive of Newtonianist ideas. Pope, as we have seen, made use of them as a platform for a critique of the knowledge-making abilities of humankind. In the Newton-heavy poetry of James Thomson, especially that of *The Seasons*, natural philosophy helped 'define implicitly the potentials of poetic imagination'.[71] Similarly, Mark Akenside's *The Pleasures of the Imagination* characterises artistic genius in terms of being able to 'scan the secret laws / Which bind them to each other', by which Newton, in Akenside's words, had finally replaced 'Fables with wonder'.[72]

The potential for poetry to be receptive of Newton's ideas is relatively well documented, and so is that of drama, especially in the studies by Coppola and Chico. It is now necessary to shift our attention to prose narrative since surprisingly little attention has been dedicated to identifying its interplay with Newtonianism. Some studies have focused on specific episodes, such as Swift's satire of Newtonian science in the third book of *Gulliver's Travels*.[73] Important works such as Lynall's *Swift and Science* mapped out the theological and political resonances of Newton's thought in Swift's works and, more broadly, in the early eighteenth-century public imagination. Points of convergence have also been identified between Newtonian theories and the novel. Notable examples include G.J. Barker-Benfield's examination of the relationship between Newton-inspired physiology and sentimental novels; Joseph Drury's contention that the establishment of the eighteenth-century novel as a machine owes much to experimental science, including of course that by Newton;

---

70   William Powell Jones, 'Newton Further Demands the Muse', *Studies in English Literature, 1500–1900*, 3 (1963), 287–306 (pp. 288–289).

71   Michael G. Ketcham, 'Scientific and Poetic Imagination in James Thomson's "Poem Sacred to the Memory of Sir Isaac Newton"', *Philological Quarterly*, 61 (1982), 33–50 (p. 33).

72   In Tindal Kareem, p. 132.

73   Milton Millhauser, 'Dr. Newton and Mr. Hyde: Scientists in Fiction from Swift to Stevenson', *Nineteenth-Century Fiction*, 28 (1973), 287–304 (pp. 289–290).

and Rivka Swenson's exploration of the dialectics of gender and Newtonian optics in Eliza Haywood's *Anti-Pamela* (1741).[74]

However, these studies do not tackle prose narrative across different authors, nor do they consider Newtonianism as an epistemological phenomenon. I have argued in this chapter that, as Newton's ideas were received and processed by his commentators, knowledge based on one's own imagination was deemed unreliable by some compared to that produced by reason. Yet, as I have also shown, there were strong objections to the claim that Newton's reason could be extended to anybody. Newton's image as an unparalleled genius made for a lofty knowledge-making standard, one which led to difficult questions about whether human abilities were enough to make sense of a nature whose laws are universal and immutable, but mysterious in their causes; and about whether there was any way for a human observer to keep the imagination in check, and apply the *hypotheses non fingo* approach like Newton had done.

In a century when, in the words of John Bender, discussions on the nature of fictionality informed scientific and literary theories, with both early scientists and early novelists advocating a 'denial of fictionality', it is likely for these questions to have found their way in eighteenth-century prose narrative too.[75] As I proceed to show in the next three chapters, they did so in rather oblique fashion, possibly because of the convoluted nature of prose narrative in eighteenth-century British culture. The works of the authors examined in this study – Daniel Defoe, Henry Fielding and David Hume – testify to the character of eighteenth-century prose narrative as a hybrid product. The nature of prose narrative at this time, which is perhaps best defined as an inchoate, experimental process in which the categories of romance, novel, history and biography tended to overlap and cross-contaminate, leads to a problematization of

---

74   G. J. Barker-Benfield, *The Culture of Sensibility: Sex and Society in Eighteenth-Century Britain* (Chicago: University of Chicago Press, 1992); Joseph Drury, *Novel Machines: Technology and Narrative Form in Enlightenment Britain* (Oxford: Oxford University Press, 2017); Rivka Swenson, 'Optics, Gender, and the Eighteenth-Century Gaze: Looking at Eliza Haywood's Anti-Pamela', *The Eighteenth Century*, 51 (2010), 27–43.

75   John Bender, 'Enlightenment Fiction and the Scientific Hypothesis', *Representations*, 60 (1997), 1–23 (p. 10).

generic and disciplinary boundaries between what are traditionally considered as fiction and non-fiction works.[76]

And yet, for all their differences, Defoe, Fielding and Hume share a receptiveness to the epistemological questions of Newtonianism discussed in this chapter. Works such as *A Journal of the Plague Year*, *Tom Jones* and the ancient England volumes of the *History of England* endorse, question or dramatize the Newtonianist confidence in the knowledge-making ability of man. In particular, I claim that Defoe, Fielding and Hume used prose narrative as a platform to explore the epistemological ramifications of Newtonianism in relation to what they believed were the correct uses of the imagination in complex knowledge-making situations, as well as to what counted as certain knowledge. It will be shown that narrators of these works regularly engage in commentaries on the processes of knowledge acquisition about complex natural, social or cultural phenomena, and constantly reflect on the processes whereby knowledge is made and spread, especially when it comes to tell reliable from spurious information.

Ultimately, as the next chapters will show, Defoe, Fielding and Hume addressed one key question which had stemmed from the diffusion of Newtonianism in British culture, and which was crucial to reflections on prose narrative as a reliable medium for transmitting knowledge: namely, whether the ability to restrain the imagination which had been ascribed to Newton was one that could be cultivated by others. They did not necessarily do so because they had read Newton's works first-hand or the popularisations of his ideas, though, as we will see, external and internal evidence suggests that all of them were interested in natural philosophy, and might have read some of the commentaries on Newton then available. More importantly, however, they did so because they partook in the climate of thought of Newtonianism which resulted from the body of commentaries on Newton and which, over time, permeated the intellectual climate of eighteenth-century British culture.

---

76   Bradbury, p. 29.

CHAPTER 3
THE UNCERTAINTY OF THINGS
The Critique of Conjectures in Defoe's
A Journal of the Plague Year

3.1. *Dealing with Invisible Natural Phenomena: The 1665 Great Plague*

In 1713, the second edition of *Principia* was published with the crucial addition of the *General Scholium*. In this new section, Newton expatiated on the workings of gravity. The 'laws of motion and the law of gravity have been found by this method' – i.e., the method of analysis and synthesis (see Chapter 1) – but to those who might object that his approach bypassed the issue of what gravity actually was, Newton offered a memorably vague response: *satis est quod gravitas revera existat*, or, in Anne Whitman's verbatim translation – 'it is enough that gravity really exists'.[1]

The rationale of this approach lies in the methodological contention that effects can be linked to causes even if we cannot figure out exactly what these causes are. Unless one has verifiable data at their disposal, explanations of the causes of invisible phenomena should never be attempted because doing so would mean coming up with so-called 'occult causes' – a term then disparagingly associated with Aristotelianism.[2] As Cotes clarifies in the editor's preface, also

---

1   Newton, *Principia*, p. 943. Some twenty years earlier, in a reply on the cause of gravity to clergyman Richard Bentley, who was preparing the first of his 1692 Boyle Lectures on God and natural philosophy, Newton wrote: 'You sometimes speak of gravity as essential and inherent to matter', Newton writes. 'Pray, do not ascribe that notion to me; for the cause of gravity is what I do not pretend to know'. In Isaac Newton, *Correspondence of Isaac Newton*, ed. by H.W. Turnbull (Cambridge: Cambridge University Press, 1963), III, 240.

2   See Keith Hutchinson, 'What Happened to Occult Qualities in the Scientific Revolution', *Isis*, 73 (1982), 233–253.

added to the second edition of *Principia*, occult causes are to be avoided because they are the offspring of the imagination:

> occult causes are not those causes whose existence is very clearly demonstrated by observations, but only those whose existence is occult, imagined, and not yet proved [...] occult causes are the refuge of those who assign the governing of these motions to some sort of vortices of a certain matter utterly fictitious and completely imperceptible to the senses.[3]

Less than a decade afterwards, Daniel Defoe also grappled with an invisible entity, one whose causes were unknown, but, different to gravity, one so deadly that it put received ideas on knowledge and society in crisis. This entity was plague. Published in 1722, Defoe's *A Journal of the Plague Year* is, according to its title page, the true history of the spreading of the 1665 Great Plague 'written by a Citizen who continued all the while in London'.[4] The *Journal* was one of the many responses to a plague scare in 1720, when pestilence struck Marseilles and menaced to reach London by maritime routes. Since the *Journal* treated of the 1665 outbreak, however, it was received by many as a true account of that event, so much so that it appears as a source in a medical treatise by physician Richard Mead (of whom more will be said later).[5]

In the early modern era, plague struck England, and London especially, on a regular basis, with memorable outbreaks having occurred in 1563, 1593, 1603 and 1625.[6] Yet, familiarity with the disease proved unhelpful in countering it, as the workings of plague

---

3   Cotes, 'Editor's Preface', p. 392.

4   Daniel Defoe, *A Journal of the Plague Year*, ed. by Paula Backscheider (New York and London: W. W. Norton and Company, 1992), p. 3. The page number of the next quotations from the *Journal* will be cited parenthetically in the body of the text.

5   Robert Mayer, 'The Reception of *A Journal of the Plague Year* and the Nexus of Fiction and History in the Novel', *ELH*, 57 (1990), 529–555 (p. 532). See also Frank Bastian, 'Defoe's *Journal of the Plague Year* Reconsidered', *The Review of English Studies*, 16 (1965), 151–173 (p. 152); Manuel Schonhorn, 'Defoe's *Journal of the Plague Year*. Topography and Intention', *The Review of English Studies*, 19 (1968), 387–402 (p. 393).

6   Ernest B. Gilman, *Plague Writing in Early Modern England* (Chicago and London: University of Chicago Press, 2009), p. 35.

were still shrouded in mystery.[7] While experience had provided ways of mitigating its impact, plague remained an event that radically altered the lives of people.[8] The high mortality rate, the rapidity of the contagion, and the difficulty in detecting its marks and restraining the infection were all factors which contributed to making plague a disease of unprecedented relevance not solely on biological terms, but also in cultural ones. 'No other disease', Rebecca Totaro remarks, 'altered physical, social, religious, medical, and civic behavior and beliefs at once'.[9] Part of a group of natural calamities like storms, earthquakes, fires and comets which, 'with their awesome power of destruction, raised questions about the cosmic plan generally and their meaning for man particularly', plague, Louis Landa notes, was unique in its disruptive potential.[10] Its ability to 'collapse boundaries between apparently disparate elements of human experience and its representation in discourse', according to Geoffrey Payne, made it the most feared natural catastrophe.[11]

Each outbreak killed people by the tens of thousands, but the 1665 Great Plague had been particularly pernicious, with a death toll of approximately 100,000 people. It had been the last major epidemic for some sixty years, at least officially, but its memory was very much alive when in 1720 Londoners heard of a plague outbreak in Marseille.[12] Concern mounted about London-bound ships sailing

---

7   Ronald Hutton, The Restoration. *A Political and Religious History of England and Wales. 1658–1667* (Oxford: Clarendon Press, 1985), p. 225.

8   Hutton, p. 230.

9   Rebecca Totaro, 'Introduction', *Representing the Plague in Early Modern England*, ed. by Rebecca Totaro and Ernest B. Gilman (New York and London: Routledge, 2010), pp. 1-15 (p. 4).

10   Louis A. Landa, 'Religion, Science, and Medicine in *A Journal of the Plague Year*', in Daniel Defoe, *A Journal of the Plague Year*, ed. by Paula Backscheider (New York and London: W. W. Norton and Company, 1992), pp. 267–285 (p. 273).

11   Geoffrey Payne, 'Distemper, Scourge, Invader: Discourse and Plague in Defoe's *A Journal of the Plague Year*', *English Studies*, 5 (2014), 620–636 (pp. 623–624).

12   The last reported case of plague in the London bills of mortality dated back to 1679, but demographic evidence on deaths in the decades since displays a statistical deviation much larger than the standard variation expected by comparing London mortality to that of the rest of the country. This suggests that it was only by the late 1720s that plague disappeared from England. See

from there. As Cindy Ermus notes, the Marseilles epidemic struck at a time when 'ideas about contagion and the usefulness of quarantine were very much in flux', and this was especially true in England.[13] Even a quick glance at the newspapers of 1721–1722, Robert Mayer notes, reveals that 'in the same pages in which medical developments on the continent were detailed, a number of books concerning the plague were advertised repeatedly'.[14] The plague scare caused disquiet in England and induced the publication of a number of medical treatises on plague, some of which were reprints from 1665. While all treatises tended to acknowledge that the epidemic was a punishment from God for various forms of misbehaviour, many of these treatises tried to understand the disease in medical terms.[15] According to Paul Slack, of the forty-six publications on plague that had been published in 1665 and 1666, some two thirds 'dealt directly with the natural causes of plague, with natural remedies or with the incidence of disease'.[16] On top of these reissues, about fifteen more treatises were published in 1721–1722, including some by renowned physicians like Richard Blackmore, Richard Mead and Hans Sloane.[17]

Given that the plague often did not display any symptoms in the first days of contagion and its workings were unknown – the bacillus responsible for the disease, *Yersinia Pestis*, and the vector of transmission, the black rat, were only discovered in 1893 – physicians had traditionally been inclined to speculate about its causes. A look at the theories on the origins of plague proposed by medical experts in the aftermath to the 1665 Great Plague shows that imaginative conjectures, the likes Newton would condemn as

---

Neil Cummins, Morgan Kelly, Cormac Ó Gráda, 'Living Standards and Plague in London, 1650–1665', *Economic History Review*, 69 (2016), 3–34 (p. 5).

13   Cindy Ermus, *The Great Plague Scare of 1720: Disaster and Diplomacy in the Eighteenth-Century Atlantic World* (Cambridge: Cambridge University Press, 2023), p. 104.

14   Mayer, p. 531.

15   Landa, p. 270.

16   Paul Slack, *The Impact of Plague in Tudor and Stuart England* (Oxford: Clarendon Press, 1985), pp. 244–245.

17   A full list of plague-related publication in 1720–1722 is available in Ermus, pp. 120–121n59.

detrimental to philosophical enquiries, were very much the norm. In the oft-reprinted *Loimologia* (1672), Nathaniel Hodges supposed that the cause of plague was an invisible 'nitrous spirit' in the human body.[18] In 1685, Robert Boyle was invited to set down his 'Thoughts and Observations by way of Conjectures' ('which I was made to believe would appear uncommon', he adds), and penned his own personal 'Theory of Diseases'. In the book, which came to be titled *Experimental Discourse of some Unheeded Causes of the Insalubrity and Salubrity of the Air*, Boyle contends that 'it seems probable that in divers places, the Salubrity and Insalubrity of the Air considered in the general, may be in good part due to subterraneal Expirations'. On plague specifically, Boyle claimed that it is caused by 'poisonous Expirations or wandering Corpuscles', clearly revealing that his conjectural approach rested on corpuscular philosophy.[19]

The situation appeared to change in the early eighteenth century. The general public was becoming increasingly familiar with the concept of empirical observation, so approaches to disease containment started to take verifiable data into account.[20] Sudden violent deaths caused by diseases started to be explained not just by divine providence, as it had been traditionally done, but also by cause-effect links based on mechanical philosophy. Although the theories formulated to account for the means of contagion of the plague were various, treatises on the plague were by and large divided into two groups: contagionists and anti-contagionists.[21]

---

18   Nathaniel Hodges, *Loimologia: or, an Historical Account of the Plague in London in 1665* (London: E. Bell and J. Osborn, 1720), p. 43.

19   Robert Boyle, *Experimental Discourse of Some Unheeded Causes of the Insalubrity and Salubrity of the Air*, annexed to *An Essay of the Great Effects of Even Languid and Unheeded Motion* (London: Richard Davis, 1685), pp. ii, 4–5, 66. On Boyle's corpuscular philosophy, see Helen Thompson, '"It was Impossible to Know These People": Secondary Qualities and the Form of Character in *A Journal of the Plague Year*', *The Eighteenth Century*, 54 (2013), 153–167 (p. 155).

20   In 1724, for instance, James Jurin compared mortality rates to assess the effectiveness of smallpox inoculation. Wayne Wild, '"Due Preparations": Defoe, Dr Mead and the Threat of Plague', *Liberating Medicine, 1720–1835*, ed. by Tristanne Connolly and Steve Clark (London: Pickering & Chatto, 2009), pp. 55–69 (pp. 56, 63n33).

21   Ermus, p. 104.

The former were the most influential group, and many of them were influenced by Newtonianism in various ways, either by direct contact with Newton's circles or by having studied at a university where Newtonian science was taught.[22] This group of physicians, which included Richard Mead, James Keill, James Jurin and Henry Pemberton, was particularly influent in the 1710s and 1720s. Mead, a former student of Newtonian physician Archbald Pitcairne, was the most important of the group. As arguably the best-respected British physician of the 1720s – he was personal doctor to Queen Anne and prime minister Robert Walpole, as well as to Newton himself – he became influential with his efforts to 'Newtonianize medicine'.[23] He did so by using Newton's quotations as an authority to establish an iatro-mechanical doctrine which held that bodily and disease processes were always due to underlying physical causes.[24]

As a result of the spread of Newtonianism, physicians who wrote about the 1720 plague scare started to acknowledge the perils of the imagination when speculating about the nature of invisible diseases. In the preface to his *Discourse on Pestilence* (1721), Richard Blackmore railed against those 'Enthusiasts in Physick' who 'conceal their notions' in 'odd Metaphors' and 'affected Obscurity'.[25] Peter Kennedy, in *A Discourse on Pestilence and Contagion in General* (1721), condemned those who, notwithstanding plague being 'difficult to determine (because of Magnitude insufficient for our Senses to discover)', kept on coming up with hypotheses.[26] Following Newton's approach with invisible phenomena like gravity, these physicians approached disease in the more cautious terms of the 'how' rather than the 'why', because they did not want

---

22 Tristanne Connolly and Steve Clark, 'Introduction', *Liberating Medicine, 1720–1835*, ed. by Tristanne Connolly and Steve Clark (London: Pickering & Chatto, 2009), pp. 1–10 (p. 3).

23 Theodore M. Brown, 'Medicine in the Shadow of the *Principia*', *Journal of the History of Ideas*, 48 (1987), 629–648 (p. 636).

24 See Arnold Zuckerman, 'Plague and Contagionism in Eighteenth-Century England: The Role of Richard Mead', *Bulletin of the History of Medicine*, 78 (2004), 273–308.

25 Richard Blackmore, *A Discourse upon the Plague, with a Preparatory Account of Malignant Fevers* (London: John Clark, 1721), p. 4.

26 Peter Kennedy, *A Discourse on Pestilence and Contagion in General; Containing the Cause, Prevention, and Cure* (London, 1721), p. 10.

to risk producing conjectural knowledge and thus let the imagination distort their knowledge about plague.[27]

And yet, possibly because of the invisible nature of plague, those very physicians could not help but feigning conjectures on certain occasions. Thus, Kennedy promoted his own theory that the disease is 'very reasonably' occasioned by 'the Complication of such malign Atoms as will necessarily come from these Bodies', together with 'unnatural Warmth' and the 'Disposition of the Air'.[28] Blackmore, on his part, imagines plague as consisting in 'the greatest Contrariety of Pestilential Vapours or Particles to the Animal Spirits, and the active Principles of the Blood, and that the first is founded in greatest Minuteness, Exaltation and Refinement'.[29]

Even Mead himself, for all his Newtonianism, still dabbled into conjectural interpretations of the disease.[30] In *A Short Discourse Concerning Pestilential Contagion, and the Methods to be used to Prevent it* (1720), he took fellow physicians to task for having feigned hypotheses, and he does so in clearly Newtonian terms. To the 'common Opinion, and propagated by Authors of great Name, that we are usually visited with the Plague once in 30 or 40 Years', he responded that it is 'a mere Fancy without any Foundation either in Reason or Experience: and therefore People ought to be delivered from the Subjection to such vain Fears'.[31] But a few pages later, Mead claims that plague formed 'an *Infectious Matter* capable of conveying the Mischief to a great Distance from the diseased Body, out of which it was produced', and that plague resided 'in Goods of a loose and soft Texture', a claim which can only be defined as speculative given the lack of verifiable observation to accompany it.[32]

---

27   Craig Spence, *Accidents and Violent Death in Early Modern London, 1650–1750* (Woodbridge: The Boydell Press, 2016), p. 7.

28   Kennedy, p. 10.

29   Blackmore, p. 5.

30   Brown, p. 636.

31   Richard Mead, *A Short Discourse Concerning Pestilential Contagion: and the Methods to be Used to Prevent It* (London: Sam. Buckley and Ralph Smith, 1720), p. 5.

32   Mead, pp. 13, 18.

The likes of Mead were highly influential in orienting the public provisions on how to tackle plague outbreaks, including which quarantine measures were to be enforced. In 1710, worrying news from Prussia and the Baltic led Queen Anne to promulgate the first Quarantine Act, which instated mandatory isolation of forty days for ships coming from unsafe areas.[33] This act was informed by the theories of contagionist physicians, as was the new Quarantine Act drafted in 1721 to supersede it. As a matter of fact, Mead's *Short Discourse* had been written at the request of Walpole for the very purpose of gathering information for the new Quarantine Act.[34] In the up-to-date bill, not only were people from an infected ship required to spend forty days in isolation; force could also be used to prevent a ship coming from an infected area from entering an English port. Withholding information on plague infection was deemed a felony and resulted in the death penalty.[35]

As a journalist involved (overtly or covertly) in at least nine periodicals at the time, Defoe was one of the most active commentators on the 1720 plague scare, mostly to criticize the anti-contagion decisions made by the government.[36] Accordingly, Defoe's polemical attacks were also levelled at the contagionist physicians who had speculated about the nature of plague. In a short book titled *Due Preparations for the Plague, as Well for Soul as Body* (1721), which was published three months before the *Journal* in response to the 1721 Quarantine Act, Defoe expressed the hope that the population put themselves 'in a posture not to be surprised' were pestilence to strike again.[37] In particular, he advised against heeding to the misleading interpretations offered by 'some physicians':

---

33   Ermus, p. 105.

34   Wild, p. 55.

35   Ermus, p. 110.

36   Paula Backscheider, 'Introduction', in Defoe, *Journal*, p. ix. On Defoe's commentary on the actions of the government, see Slack, pp. 326–327. Defoe's first comments on the plague dated back at least to 1709. See Landa, p. 271.

37   Travis Chi Wing Lau, 'Defoe Before Immunity: A Prophylactic *Journal of the Plague Year*', *Digital Defoe: Studies in Defoe & His Contemporaries*, 8 (2016), 23–39 (p. 25).

who have given their opinions in the matter of our managing ourselves with respect to medicine, in case of the plague breaking out among us, and unto this purpose they treat a little (though very superficially) of the nature of the disease. [...] yet they differ with, contradict, and oppose one another, and leave their readers as uncertain and dissatisfied, as far to seek, and at a loss for their conduct, as they were before.[38]

Defoe's interest in how people made sense of plague was linked to a broader cultural interest in the explanatory possibilities offered by medicine and experimental science. His plague-related interventions occurred within a 'common lay and medical culture' in which it was widely believed that 'one could diagnose and treat illness'.[39] While Defoe's interest in medicine is well documented, his interventions on plague may also be linked to knowledge of Newton's ideas.[40] External evidence is not conclusive; what we know from Defoe's library holdings is that they were auctioned off in 1731 along with those of Mr Phillips Farewell, a clergyman, so there is no way of knowing for certain if the texts by Newton (the third edition of *Principia* published in 1726) and the two popularizations by Whiston, *Praelectiones Astronomicae* (1707) and *Praelectiones Physico-Mathematicae* (1726) were Defoe's.[41] But internal evidence in his works does point to familiarity with some of the elements of Newtonian science. In *A General History of the Discoveries and Improvements in the Useful Arts* (1725–1727), for example, Defoe states that: 'Sir *Isaac Newton* demonstrates that Gravity is a very different thing from *Magnetism*, since the former is always as the quantity of Matter attracted, but *Magnetism* by no

---

38   Daniel Defoe, *Due Preparations for the Plague, as Well for Soul and Body* (London: E: Matthews and J. Batley, 1722), p. 5.

39   Andrew Wear, 'Introduction', Daniel Defoe, *Due Preparations for the Plague, As well for Soul and Body*, ed. by Andrew Wear (London: Pickering & Chatto, 2002), pp. 1–20 (p. 12).

40   On Defoe and medicine, see Geoffrey Sill, *The Cure of the Passions and the Origins of the English Novel* (Cambridge: Cambridge University Press, 2001), pp. 69–85.

41   Ilse Vickers, *Defoe and the New Sciences* (Cambridge: Cambridge University Press, 1996), pp. 177–181.

means so'.[42] A passage of *The Compleat English Gentleman* (1729) has Defoe claim that the ideal citizen of the English polity ought to take a 'whole course of Philosophy', a key part of it being reading 'all that Sir Isaac Newton [...] had said upon the nicest subjects in Astronomy and the secrets of nature'.[43]

That Defoe was acquainted with Newtonian science is not that surprising if one considers that his education took place at Newington Green academy, where both the experimental philosophy of the Royal Society practitioners and the French corpuscular theorists of Descartes and Pierre Gassendi were taught.[44] It is not easy to establish the actual extent of Defoe's familiarity with Newton, but, as I examined in a separate contribution, the frequency of references to mathematical demonstration in *The Consolidator* (1705) points to Defoe's awareness that an epistemological shift had occurred after Newton.[45] In this work in which a traveler embarks on a journey to the moon (a satirical double for England), not only is Newton explicitly named alongside Boyle as a paragon of scientific thinking, but the lunar inhabitants are also characterized as beings who can calculate everything, including invisible entities. For instance, they are able to compute the 'regular and irregular Motions' of the winds, as well as 'its Compositions and Quantities; from whence, by a sort of Algebra, they can cast up its Duration, Violence, and Extent: In these Calculations, some say, those Authors have been so exact, that they can, as our Philosophers say of Comets, state their Revolutions'.[46]

---

42   Daniel Defoe, *A General History of Discoveries and Improvements, in Useful Arts, Particularly in the Great Branches of Commerce, Navigation, and Plantation* (London: J. Roberts, 1726), pp. 257–258; see Maximillian E. Novak, *Daniel Defoe Master of Fiction: His Life and Works* (Oxford: Oxford University Press, 2011), p. 646.

43   Daniel Defoe, *The Compleat English Gentleman*, ed. by Karl D. Bülbring (London: D. Nutt, 1890), p. 207.

44   Vickers, p. 80. See also Lew Girdler, 'Defoe's Education at Newington Green Academy', *Studies in Philology*, 50 (1953), 573–591.

45   Alessio Mattana, '"The Eye to the Object": The Question of Demonstrative Knowledge in Defoe's *The Consolidator*', *English Studies*, 104 (2023), 677–694.

46   Daniel, Defoe, *The Consolidator*, ed. by Michael Seidel, Maximillian E. Novak, and Joyce D. Kennedy (New York: AMS Press, 2001), p. 6.

These preliminary remarks are critical for our examination of *A Journal of the Plague Year*, a narrative work in which Defoe describes life in London during the 1665 Great Plague epidemic from the perspective of a survivor. Published as a complementary piece to *Due Preparations*, the *Journal*, in the word of a commentator, displays a 'sustained engagement between the existence of the plague and the structures of medical institutions' in order to make the plague into a natural phenomenon which can be 'subjected to the ordering structures of science'.[47] In the following sections of this chapter, this claim is problematized by investigating the ways in which the *Journal* partakes in the Newtonianist challenge to conjecture-making. Via a set of explicit and implicit evaluations on the accepted ways of producing knowledge about plague, Defoe's narrator and main character H.F. conveys scepticism about medical knowledge and, indeed, about any other framework of explanation. Defoe's interrogation of the 1665 outbreak is conducted with the two-fold goal of assessing the consequences of the unverified, fantastic reports about plague that circulated in London in 1665; and understanding if, and how, accurate knowledge could be produced in case of a new outbreak.

As it will also be argued, a significant aspect of the *Journal* is that Defoe's interrogation of the epistemology of plague is carried out by fictional means. Defoe did not experience the Great Plague first-hand as he was only five years old at the time of the outbreak. Although the *Journal* is replete with references to topical circumstances, which were aimed at criticizing the decisions made by the government in point of plague prevention, Defoe's choice to set his account in 1665, and the adoption of a fictional narrator, hint at a voluntary disregard of topicality. It has been noted that in the *Journal* Defoe oscillates between particular observations on how plague works and more general observations on human nature.[48] Building on this view, it is finally claimed in this chapter that Defoe's goal in the *Journal* is to construct an epistemological scenario, one in which plague was an

---

47 Payne, pp. 623–624.
48 David Roberts, 'Introduction', Daniel Defoe, *A Journal of the Plague Year*, ed. by David Roberts (Oxford: Oxford University Press, 2010), pp. 10–29 (p. 24).

extreme case study to gauge how reliable human-made knowledge could be when dealing with an invisible, deadly natural catastrophe which offered almost no information about its workings. To the examination of these arguments the next sections now turn.

3.2. *The Attack on Conjectures in the Journal*

From the very first few pages of the *Journal*, Defoe's focus is on the way a set of ill-grounded conjectures delayed the realisation that plague had broken out in London. The narrative begins before the first cases of contagion have even occurred. H.F. states that 'it was about the Beginning of *September* 1664, that I, among the Rest of my Neighbours, heard in ordinary Discourse, that the Plague was return'd again in Holland' (p. 5). Speculations arose on where the disease had arrived from: 'some said from *Italy*, others from the *Levant* […]; others said it was brought from *Candia*; others from *Cyprus*' (p. 5). In those days, H.F. adds, information circulated by 'Word of Mouth', which in turn generated 'Rumours and Reports of Things' (p. 6).

Months later, two men, 'said to be French-men', were found dead just outside London at the beginning of December 1664 (pp. 5–6). City officers received a report of their death from an unverified source, upon which an enquiry was made 'in order to be certain of the truth' (p. 6) and determine whether they had died by plague or another infection. This task was conducted by two physicians and a surgeon, who, as outlined in the *Order of Health* (the provisions to deal with the contagion issued by the London Mayor in 1665 and annexed almost verbatim to the *Journal*), were the professionals designated to discern the presence of plague in dubious cases. Their role was 'to join the Searchers for the view of the Body, to the end that there may be a true Report made of the Disease' – that is, to distinguish the marks of plague in suspected bodies and authenticate them, a measure that, as H.F. clarifies, was made necessary by the 'great abuse in misreporting the Disease' (p. 37). Their inspection was concluded with the discovery of 'evident Tokens of the Sickness upon both the Bodies', upon which the physicians and the surgeon gave 'their Opinions publickly' (p. 6) that the two Frenchmen had died by plague. This piece of information was then conveyed to the parish clerk, who in turn spread it 'by Word of Mouth' to his parishioners, and was eventually published in the so-called 'Bills of Mortality', the weekly list of those who died in each London parish sorted by cause of demise, which were then publicly affixed across the city (p. 6).

With two persons now officially dead by plague, Londoners 'began to be allarm'd all over the Town', and even more so after the death of 'another Man […] in the same House, and of the same Distemper' at the end of December (p. 6). But in the following six weeks 'nobody died with any Marks of Infection', and since the bills of Mortality did not mention any more victims of plague, people assumed that 'the Distemper was gone' (p. 6). H.F. specifies that this last piece of information also came to be produced in an unreliable way – 'It was said' is, once again, his word choice. That the plague had subsided was a supposition soon subverted by another death in mid-February, 'in another House, but in the same Parish, and in the same manner'. This last occurrence

> turn'd the People[']s Eyes pretty much towards that End of the Town; and the weekly Bills showing an Encrease of Burials in St. *Giles's* Parish more than usual, it began to be suspected, that the Plague was among the People at that End of the Town' (p. 6).

People inferred that the death toll was higher than authorities reported, because the latter 'had taken Care to keep it as much from the Knowledge of the Publick'. This supposition, H.F. notes, 'possess'd the Heads of the People very much' (p. 6), and many interpreted the marked increase in the overall count of burials in the parish of St Giles as a sign of pestilence. As the number of victims decreased again, 'every body began to look upon the Danger as good as over', notwithstanding the persistently high number of burials in the parish of St. Giles and a more than suspicious number of people who 'died of the Spotted-Feaver' (p. 8), an event that should have led people to acknowledge that they were already in the middle of an outbreak.

These few introductory pages reveal a complex network of assumptions regarding the onset of the 1665 plague outbreak. The Londoners described by H.F. eventually settled for the mistaken idea that the unexplained deaths had not been due to plague but to some other disease. Even if they were guilty of believing 'word-of-mouth' information somewhat too easily, they still did so in good faith. Their belief was based on three pieces of conjectural knowledge: namely, that the bodily marks found on the corpses were the necessary sign of pestilence; that the absence of bodily marks meant no plague; and that the bills of mortality accurately mapped the diffusion of the disease. Each of these assumptions had a fairly high probability of being true. The first was plausible because the marks on the bodies of the sick were confirmed by the public authority. The second logically follows from the first: if plague is identifiable by its bodily marks, then their absence must mean no disease. The third, finally, is grounded on the bills of mortality being the method officially employed by the London officers to track the spread of diseases.

For all their likelihood, these conjectures were undermined by the lack of certain information on how bodily marks appear following a plague infection. We now know that bubonic plague acts inconspicuously for the first three days of contagion, and the 'buboes', the circular signs typical of the disease, tend to appear later in the course of the infection.[49] This was not known in 1665, nor in 1722. At the time, one could only make suppositions grounded on the trustworthiness of those appointed to detect the signs of the plague. These people, however, had little or no medical expertise. According to the *Orders for Health*, infections were to be certified by physicians. Yet, the first detection activities were actually carried out by the 'Searchers', lay examiners chosen amongst 'Persons of good Sort and Credit'. The searchers, H.F. writes, mainly included elderly women of 'honest reputation', who were sworn 'to make due Search, and true Report' (p. 36) and were assigned the task of

---

49   A. Lloyd Moote and Dorothy C. Moote, *The Great Plague: The Story of London's Most Deadly Year* (Baltimore and London: Johns Hopkins University Press, 2004), pp. 62–63. See also Jayne Elizabeth Lewis, 'Spectral Currencies in the Air of Reality: *A Journal of the Plague Year* and the History of Apparitions', *Representations*, 87 (2004), 82–101 (p. 84).

travelling from house to house to record cases of infection and death by plague.[50]

Defoe had reservations on the employment of women searchers. In an issue of the *Applebee Journal* published in November 1722, a few months after the *Journal*, he would denounce their 'ignorance' and the 'slight Inquiries they make after the Fact'.[51] This accusation was a common one. The women searchers were regularly accused of wanting medical expertise, as well as of having poor morals, with stories circulating about their taking bribes to help infected people avoid being quarantined.[52] Mead, who had levelled similar accusations, proposed that 'understanding' and 'diligent' men be appointed for the role in the stead of women.[53] However, the problem ran much deeper than replacing women searchers. Regardless of who carried out the search, not enough was known of the plague to establish who was sick and who was not, and this was compounded by drastically low levels of literacy, which led most lay people to rely on second-hand knowledge about infections. As Craig Spence puts it, tragic events such as plague were 'socially amplified by a dynamic mixture of judicial theatre, oral repetition and printed dissemination', all of which created distortions in the perception of people.[54]

Significantly, in the *Journal* Londoners are routinely portrayed in the act of interpreting plague in erroneous ways due to their rampant imagination. During one of his solitary peregrinations through of the city, H.F. finds a group of people intent at staring up into the air, 'to see what a Woman told them appeared plain to her, which was an Angel cloth'd in white, with a fiery Sword in his Hand, waving it, or

---

50 Jacob Murel, 'Print, Authority, and the Bills of Mortality in Seventeenth-Century London', *The Seventeenth Century*, 36 (2021), 1–25 (p. 2).

51 In Paula McDowell, 'Defoe and the Contagion of the Oral: Modeling Media Shift in *A Journal of the Plague Year*', *PMLA*, 121 (2006), 87–106 (p. 98).

52 Murel, p. 2.

53 Wanda S. Henry, 'Women Searchers of the Dead in Eighteenth- and Nineteenth-Century London', *Social History of Medicine*, 29 (2016), 445–466 (pp. 450–1). Henry has also shown from demographic data that most London parishes in the first half of the eighteenth century did appoint women, but not all of them were elderly.

54 Spence, pp. 215–216.

brandishing it over his Head'. Her description, complete in 'every Part of the Figure', even its motions, convinces the whole group: a man sees 'it all plainly' and recognizes the sword 'as plain as can be'; another sees the angel; yet another one his face. H.F., though looking 'as earnestly as the rest', cannot see anything (p. 23).

His conclusion is that these sights are due to the corrupting influence of the imagination. When he tells the story of the old women who interpreted other people's dreams as omens of the pestilence, his argument against such practices is that the interference of the imagination distorts the senses of people. As a result, they convince themselves, and persuade one other, that they are seeing 'Shapes and Figures, Representations and Appearances' (p. 22) in lieu of regular sights. These people, H.F. notes:

> Heard Voices that never spake, and saw Sights that never appear'd; but the Imagination of the people was really turn'd wayward and possess'd; And no Wonder, if they, who were poreing continually at the Clouds, saw Shapes and Figures, Representations and Appearances, which had nothing in them, but Air and Vapour. [...] just as the Imagination of the poor terrify'd People furnish'd them with Matter to work upon. (p. 22)

As H.F. remarks, this way of producing knowledge has dire effects on society. The 'extravagant reports' on the number of casualties are 'very prejudicial to our trade, as well as unjust and injurious in themselves, for it was a long time after the plague was quite over before our trade could recover itself' (p. 169). The indirect economic effect on the life of people, though severe, is however a minor cause of concern compared to the fact that human lives are at stake whenever a decision grounded on imagination-based knowledge is taken. At the beginning of the *Journal*, H.F. reports that in the early stages of the plague outbreak, groups of people stormed the Mayor's house in order to obtain certificates of health. As a result of owning the certificates, these people were deemed sound by the authorities and could freely roam outside of the city, while the rest were barred from leaving London, where the disease threatened to grow stronger. The rush for the certificates was triggered by a false report on a provision taken by the government, which H.F. underlines had its foundation only 'in the Imagination':

> It was rumour'd that an order of the Government was to be issued out, to place Turn-pikes and Barriers on the Road, to prevent Peoples travelling; and that the Towns on the Road would not suffer People from London to pass, for fear of brining the Infection along with them, though neither of these Rumours had any Foundation, but in the Imagination. (p. 11)

On the same grounds, H.F. portrays a group of Londoners as easily convincing themselves that they were immune to plague because they trusted the talismans sold by the many quacks who tried to profit from the Great Plague. The 'mighty Fancy' of these people was 'that they should not be visited, or at least that it would not be so violent among them', and other people 'fancied' that the smell of pitch and tar 'would preserve them' (p. 93).

H.F. defines these acts of trust as 'Follies', which are all the more despicable 'in a Time of such Danger, in a matter of such Consequences as this, of a National Infection' (p. 32). Fantastical notions greatly contribute to spreading the disease and increasing the number of victims, for 'one Man' may 'give the Plague to a thousand People, and they to greater Numbers in Proportion' (p. 154). Towards the end of the *Journal*, when the infection was starting to subdue, many Londoners conjectured that 'the Infection was all in the Air, that there was no such thing as Contagion from the sick People to the Sound' and start assembling and meeting again in public places. By this unfounded supposition, labelled by H.F. as a 'Whimsy', these people facilitated a new wave of infection. Some 'paid for their audacious Boldness with the Price of their Lives', and 'an infinite Number fell sick' (p. 179).

Crucially to Defoe's argument in the *Journal*, the disruptive interference of fancy in arguments made about plague is not limited to laypersons but to medical experts too. The fictitious Dr Heath, who is modelled after some of the physicians who published theories on the cause of plague, is portrayed by H.F. as a strong advocate of the 'opinion' that pestilence 'might be known by the smell of [people's] Breath'. It is this belief, expressed by a physician, that brings people to imagine that 'living creatures [...] of strange monstrous and frightful Shapes, such as Dragons, Snakes, Serpents, and Devils' might be seen if powerful enough microscopes were deployed (p. 159). With the creation of Dr Heath, Defoe seems to adversely characterise the many physicians who came up with conjectural causes of plague infections.[55] Significantly, however, Defoe's charge is not that physicians consciously lied, but that they tried to come up with conjectures to find answers, and in so doing ended up spreading misinformation. They had relied on the faculty of imagination to explain phenomena they could not visualize, and thus produced spurious knowledge.

In a way, they had no choice, as plague does not seem to allow the possibility of avoiding conjectures altogether. H.F. himself underlines that the temptation to feign conjectures on the nature of plague arose from a necessity to make sense of a disease that left little or no reference points to understand its mechanisms and limit the rate of infection. He explains that some people 'had very little Notice of their being infected at all, till the Gangreen has spread thro' their whole Body'. And, while it was true that 'upon examining the Bodies [of the victims] after they were Dead' physicians always found 'either [the] Tokens upon them, or other evident Proofs of the Distemper', yet not even they could ever 'know certainly how it was with them, till they opened their Breasts, or other Parts of their Body, and saw the Tokens' (p. 70). In these cases, verifiability could only be reached post-mortem, too late for preventing further contagion. Moreover, the epidemic continued unabated regardless of whether people refrained from attempting to find explanations. The plague infection went on even after acknowledging that there was no way of obtaining reliable data on the disease. This exacerbated the tendency of people to come up with fantastical ideas.

---

55   On Defoe's critique of medicine in *A Journal of the Plague Year*, see Katherine E. Kickel, *Novel Notions: Medical Discourse and the Mapping of the Imagination in Eighteenth-Century English Fiction* (New York: Routledge, 2023), pp. 13–40.

3.3. *Between Fact and Fiction: The Journal as a Textual Experiment*

H.F.'s reaction to the knowledge-making conundrum described above – his being torn between the need to find explanations in order to make sense of the plague and the awareness that imagination-based conjectures will contribute to spreading inaccurate information – is to adopt a sceptical stance towards all conjectural assumptions advanced by his contemporaries. Irrespective of who formulates them, all plague-related hypotheses must be rejected because there is no way of establishing whether they are correct, no matter how creditable their utterer is.

This suspension of hypotheses, however, does not result in H.F. showing Newtonianist confidence in establishing certain knowledge. The furthest H.F. goes is avoiding disseminating erroneous plague-related knowledge, based on the idea that everything that can be said about the plague is inevitably conjectural, and truth must be deferred to a time when better knowledge is available. This sceptical attitude is displayed at numerous points in the *Journal*. When no better source than the 'Enquiry of the Neighbours' can be obtained, for instance, H.F. does not attempt to offer an alternative interpretation for a given event, but rather leaves the matter open to discussion until future observations can establish the truth of the story: '[s]eeing then that we cou'd come at the certainty of Things by no Method but that of Enquiry of the Neighbours, or of the Family, and on that we cou'd not justly depend, it was not possible, but that the uncertainty of this Matter wou'd remain as above' (p. 133).

In this regard, the benchmark of valid knowledge for H.F. is Newtonianist, in that, theoretically, his aim is nothing less than 'the certainty of Things' (p. 133), which is what H.F. repeatedly aspires to in his discussion of the Great Plague. For instance, the opinion of the fictitious Dr Heath, according to whom 'the Breath of such a Person would poison, and instantly kill a Bird', is dismissed by H.F. as part of a body of 'Opinions which I never found supported by any Experiments' (p. 157). But such a threshold is unrealistically high in a pestilence-stricken environment. Plague, H.F. points out, is an extreme case among natural phenomena because, from the perspective of a human observer, it is completely opaque:

> It is impossible in a Visitation to prevent the spreading of the Plague by the utmost human Vigilance, (viz.), […] it is impossible to know the infected People from the sound, or that the infected People should perfectly know themselves. […] for none knows when, or where, or how they have received the Infection, or from whom. (pp. 151–52)

In this situation of all-encompassing uncertainty, religion would seem the obvious framework to fall back to in order to make sense of the plague. In the *Journal*, H.F. nominally subscribes to the view that natural catastrophes are, ultimately, manifestations of God's anger: '[w]hen I am speaking of the Plague, as a Distemper arising from natural Causes', he explains, 'we must consider it as it was really propagated by natural Means, nor is it at all less a Judgment for its being under the Conduct of humane Causes and Effects' (p. 153).

However, religion plays a surprisingly limited role in the *Journal* when compared to discussions of natural causes, the bills of mortality and the provisions taken by the government to restrain the outbreak.[56] The reason is that human sinfulness is a given. Not sinning is vital for the prevention of future catastrophes, but within Defoe's voluntarist outlook, the question of what exactly provoked God's wrath remains unclear. As Robert Markley noted, in early eighteenth-century Britain the language used to make sense of natural disasters was still that of providence, but the 'apparently arbitrary nature of punishment that victimizes starving widows and children' led to difficult questions about the kind of divine retribution that was being carried out.[57] In light of this inability to fully grasp the providential design behind natural disasters, understanding how the nature of disease works was therefore as important as acknowledging the hand of providence.

---

56   Wild, p. 57.
57   Robert Markley, '"Casualties and Disasters": Defoe and the Interpretation of Climatic Instability', *Journal for Early Modern Cultural Studies*, 8 (2008), 102–124 (p. 109).

This should not be taken to mean that Defoe's goal is attaining a degree of scientific objectivity in his account of the Great Plague, as W.L. Wainwright implies when he writes that H.F.'s purpose is to 'carefully assess all sorts of evidence, bear testimony to acts of virtue and vice, apparently presenting as objective a picture as possible' of plague.[58] Building on Paula Backscheider's argument that Defoe's innovation in his fiction lay not in his ability to imitate life, but in the 'imitation of reporting and imitating', a process which is meant to problematize the very concept of objectivity, we should be wary of mistaking what Defoe seems to be claiming with his representation of knowledge-making processes.[59] What is conducted in the *Journal* may be understood as a textual experiment, one in which the author depicts people as they try to make sense of a complex natural phenomenon, and the narrator as he criticizes these attempts. Significantly, throughout his narrative H.F. tries not to impose his own views in order to avoid the diffusion of ungrounded knowledge, a point also observed by Wainwright, who wrote that the *Journal*'s narrator has 'no particular angle or pet theory to push'.[60] This, however, comes with the caveat that objectivity is not sought after by Defoe, because in a plague setting like that of the Great Plague London, this goal is impossible to attain.

On the contrary, the expectation that objectivity may be reached when talking about plague is often undermined by Defoe via his mouthpiece H.F. This is apparent in the criticism of the London bills of mortality throughout the *Journal*. The bills, which had been established in 1592 to report weekly deaths divided by city parish and cause of demise, were an extremely helpful tool because, amidst unfounded information, they were felt to provide a way of tracking numerically the progress of the disease. By 'dividing up and quantifying the effects of epidemic disease', as Erin Sullivan

---

58   W. L. Wainwright, 'Lending to the Lord: Defoe's Rhetorical Design in *A Journal of the Plague Year*', *British Journal for Eighteenth-Century Studies*, 13 (1990), 59–72 (p. 61).

59   Paula R. Backscheider, *Daniel Defoe: Ambition and Innovation* (Lexington, KY: University of Kentucky Press, 1987), p. 9.

60   Wainwright, p. 61.

explains, the bills helped Londoners 'mentally track, contain, and make sense of the threat they were facing'.[61]

For these reasons, the bills were trusted as a reliable source of information on the plague. London printers regularly republished the bills from previous years, which allowed readers to grasp the progression of the disease in a way that seemed to them accurate.[62] However, even if plague was made more tangible by its being expressed numerically in the bills, the data they contained was far from objective. Their numerical values still relied on the interpretation of eyewitnesses in charge of establishing the cause of death of a person, and this method, as we discussed above, was far from conclusive.[63] Searchers were invested with the authority to see correctly 'signs that may not have been clearly visible to others', a point that, as Richelle Munkhoff insightfully notes, means that 'at the heart of the supposedly objective bills of mortality lies the searcher's interpretative function, a function that calculates ambiguous signs – tokens, botches, carbuncles – into literal figures'.[64] Such grounds were not typically questioned by city authorities, and the data collected by the searchers was taken as evidence for the bills.

We now have conclusive evidence that the bills of mortality during the 1665 epidemic were largely unreliable.[65] Defoe did not have such evidence at his disposal, but he too harboured serious reservations about the reliability of the bills. In the *Applebee Journal* in 1722, he claimed that 'nothing can be depended on from our bills of Mortality' because of the unsatisfactory enquiries made by the searchers.[66] This criticism was partly animated by Defoe's political

---

61   Erin Sullivan, 'Physical and Spiritual Illness. Narrative Appropriations of the Bills of Mortality', *Representing the Plague in Early Modern England*, ed. by Rebecca Totaro and Ernest B. Gilman (London: Routledge, 2011), pp. 76–94 (p. 76).

62   Will Slauter, 'Write up Your Dead', *Media History*, 17 (2011), 1–15 (p. 5).

63   Richelle Munkhoff, 'Searchers of the Dead: Authority, Marginality, and the Interpretation of Plague in England, 1674–1665', *Gender & History*, 11 (1999), 1–29 (pp. 8–9).

64   Munkhoff, p. 12.

65   Cummins, Kelly, Ó Gráda, p. 13.

66   In McDowell, p. 98. On Defoe and *Applebee* journal, see P.N. Furbank and W. R. Owens, 'The Myth of Defoe as *Applebee's* Man', *The Review of English Studies*, 48 (1997), 198–204; Maximillian Novak, 'Daniel Defoe and

agenda. For one, since the bills were calculated by looking at each Anglican parish in London, it was unclear whether burials of non-conformist people were recorded, so Dissenters like Defoe routinely questioned the usefulness of the bills.[67] Moreover, Defoe was critical of the way the data in the bills were used to justify isolationist policies, which in his opinion undermined England's capabilities as an economic power.[68]

On top of these political preoccupations, however, an important epistemic dimension is at play in Defoe's questioning of the validity of the bills, one which is noticeable in the *Journal*. Defoe's misgivings about the bills were due to the feeling of objectivity inherent in the numbers, which led people to mistakenly believe they had finally moved away 'from the realm of narrative and rumour to that of fact and accuracy', as Munkhoff puts it.[69] Accordingly, H.F. constantly remarks on the inaccuracy of the bills. After nine weeks of pestilence, for example, he denounces that 'there died near a thousand a-day [...] even by the Account of the weekly Bills, which yet I have Reason to be assur'd never gave a full Account', and he specifies that a mistake of 'many thousands' in the calculations was no doubt caused by lack of lucidity – 'the Confusion being such' – and imperfect sensorial conditions (p. 82). Similarly, when discussing the number of babies who died by plague, H.F. deems it necessary to clarify that though 'something of it will appear in the unusual Numbers which are put into the Weekly Bills', he is 'far from allowing them to be able to give any Thing of a full Account' (p. 96).

Once more, H.F.'s critique of the bills, which are said to 'never come at any just Account of Numbers' (p. 150), involves the grounds upon which their veracity depended. As highlighted above, H.F. claims that neither the lay searchers nor authoritative physicians should be trusted as sources.[70] This problem is compounded by the fact that

---

Applebee's Original Weekly Journal: An Attempt at Re-Attribution', *Eighteenth-Century Studies*, 45 (2012), 585–608.

67   Spence, p. 14. On the bills being used by Defoe as a way to challenge public authorities, see Murel, p. 20.

68   Wing Lau, p. 32.

69   Munkhoff, p. 13.

70   McDowell, p. 88.

the bills were printed, a process by which erroneous conjectures are propagated as objective truths, with dire consequences:

> [O]ne of the most eminent Physicians [Hodges], who has since publish'd in Latin an Account of those Times, and of his Observations, says, that in one Week there died twelve Thousand People, and that particularly there died four Thousand in one Night; tho' I do not remember that there ever was any such particular Night, so remarkably fatal, as that such a Number died in it: However, all this confirms what I have said above of the Uncertainty of the Bills of Mortality, &c. (p. 150)

As many as seventy-two single occurrences of the term 'Bills' and seventeen in-text graphic renditions can be counted in the *Journal*. As Nicholas Seager has argued, in the context of a work like the *Journal* it might seem obvious to interpret the insertion of the bills as an authentication device, one of those 'tactic[s] for lending the fiction credibility' that was employed by early novelists.[71] However, the presence of the bills might well be understood in the opposite way, as a statement 'about the fictitious nature of numerical data, a reaction to rather than an endorsement of seventeenth- and eighteenth-century quantification projects'.[72]

Fiction helps Defoe foreground his scepticism about numbers, but not because he was critical of scientific projects per se. As a reader of the *Philosophical Transactions*, we have evidence that Defoe was appreciative of efforts to gather statistical data on complex phenomena such as that made by Fellow of the Royal Society John Graunt, who in his groundbreaking *Natural and Political Observations* (1662) had inaugurated the use of the bills to track the progress of the outbreak – an activity that allowed him to deduce 'so many abstruse, and unexpected inferences out of these poor despised Bills of Mortality'.[73] Rather, by portraying H.F.'s scepticism on the

---

71   Nicholas Seager, 'Lies, Damned Lies, and Statistics: Epistemology and Fiction in Defoe's *A Journal of the Plague Year*', *Modern Language Review*, 103 (2008), 639–653 (p. 640).
72   Ibid.
73   John Graunt, *Natural and Political Observations* (London: J. Martin, 1662), p. 67.

bills, Defoe is making a statement on the impossibility of gathering certain information on a natural phenomenon such as plague, which disrupts all attempts at making knowledge. René Girard once claimed that plague is a literary trope that stands for the abrupt invalidation of all human knowledge and the ensuing impossibility to make any kind of decision.[74] As John Richetti explains, plague in early-modern England was indeed perceived as an exceptional event, in that it was the only natural catastrophe which could cast humankind in 'an extended moment of total uncertainty, an exaggerated, nearly metaphysical version provided by history of the random destructiveness of an environment'.[75] Even more so than storms and fires, the extraordinary destructive power of plague, coupled with the difficulty in understanding its causes, raised questions about man's ability to understand nature, shaking all confidence in human knowledge-making abilities.[76]

In this sense, Defoe's re-enactment of the 1665 outbreak is a choice that not only exploits historical fiction to think about the contemporary concerns of the 1720–21 plague scare, but, more importantly, serves as a narrative scenario to highlight the human struggle to produce reliable knowledge in extreme conditions. In Christopher Loar's words, Defoe offers the readers 'a way of understanding how the human can more safely inhabit often perilous environments without pretensions of mastery'.[77] Jakub Lipski has noted that in his novels Defoe tends to place his characters 'in extreme circumstances', thematizing the concept of 'isolation' with the aim of pondering 'more general questions about human nature'.[78] The *Journal* represents an extreme version of this argument, in that

---

74   René Girard, 'The Plague in Literature and Myth', *Texas Studies in Literature and Language*, 15 (1974), 833–850 (p. 835).

75   John Richetti, 'Epilogue: *A Journal of the Plague Year* as Epitome', in Daniel Defoe, *A Journal of the Plague Year*, ed. by Paula Backscheider (New York and London: W. W. Norton and Company, 1992), pp. 295–301 (p. 296).

76   Landa, p. 270.

77   Christopher F. Loar, 'Plague's Ecologies: Daniel Defoe and the Epidemic Constitution', *Eighteenth-Century Fiction*, 32 (2019), 31–53 (p. 32).

78   Jakub Lipski, 'Defoe, Cities and the Plague', *The Palgrave Encyclopedia of Urban Literary Studies*, ed. by Jeremy Tambling (London: Palgrave Macmillan, 2022), pp. 515–520 (p. 516).

Defoe creates a situation where certainty can never be achieved. Conjectures, such as those on which the bills are based, should be avoided because they offer a mistaken impression of certainty, thus fostering a false sense of security which eventually aggravates the perils of plague; and yet, they are the only way for people to make some sense of the disease.

3.4. *The Problem of Language and the Hypotheses non Fingo as Voluntary Aphasia*

If plague in the *Journal* offered a counterpoint to the Newtonianist confidence that hitherto unsolved questions about nature could be finally unveiled, the Newtonianist principle of the *hypotheses non fingo* is enacted to its extreme consequences – that of silence. When faced with a choice between assuming something or remaining silent, H.F. always opts for the latter. For example, on the story of the wickedness of the buriers, who were accused of stealing the personal items of the dead, H.F. states that 'I can only relate it and leave it undetermined' (p. 55). Similarly, while addressing the rumours about plague-stricken people infecting others, H.F. reports that some physicians speculated that the reason for this behaviour lies in the nature of the disease; others placed it 'to the Account of the Corruption of humane nature'; others still thought it was desperation. In contrast to all these views, H.F. chooses to give 'this grave Debate a quite different turn, and answer it or resolve it all by saying, that I do not grant the Fact' (p. 124). Behind these positions, one glances what Novak calls H.F.'s 'sense of the inadequacy of language'.[79] He specifies, for instance, that he cannot accept some of the stories he heard because of their linguistic imprecision, as they were not 'really true, that is to say, in the Colours they were describ'd in' (p. 124). So, while H.F. does stay silent when faced

---

79   Maximillian E. Novak, 'The Unmentionable and the Ineffable in Defoe's Fiction', *Studies in the Literary Imagination*, 15 (1982), 85–102 (p. 99).

with conjectural knowledge, he also negatively comments on words which describe plague-related events in inaccurate ways.[80]

H.F.'s incapability of 'transmitting an adequate verbal picture of the daily horrors that he sees and hears' is nowhere more evident than in his distrust of figurative language.[81] Commentators like Ilse Vickers have found connections between Defoe's wariness towards metaphorical language and the Royal Society programme for the reformation of language.[82] In the 'Manner of Discourse' chapter of his *History of the Royal Society* (1667), Thomas Sprat had expressed his misgivings towards all forms of rhetorical 'swellings of style', advocating a sustained use of language 'plainness' that translates into a voluntary relinquishment of figures of speech.[83] Defoe's general writing style might be said to have been inspired by the insistence on plain language by early scientists, but in the *Journal* something else seems to be at play. H.F. insists that the problem of figurative language is its being an improper application of one's imagination to know what cannot be directly perceived. As imaginative replacements of real objects, metaphors hinder H.F.'s goal to provide an objective, 'more perfect idea of a complicated distress'. That is why he typically chooses to stop at the threshold of the metaphorical expression, once again preferring silence over conjecture:

> I could dwell a great while upon the calamities of this dreadful time, and go on to describe the objects that appeared among us every day, [...] after I have mentioned these things, what can be added more? What can

---

80   James Cruise, '*A Journal of the Plague Year*: Defoe's Grammatology and the Secrets of Belonging', *The Eighteenth Century*, 54 (2013), 479–495 (p. 482).

81   Novak, 'The Unmentionable', p. 99.

82   Vickers, p. 39.

83   Sprat, p. 113. See also Richard Nate, '"Plain and Vulgarly Express'd": Margaret Cavendish and the Discourse of the New Science', *Rhetorica: A Journal of the History of Rhetoric*, 19 (2001), 403–417 (pp. 405–408). That said, as Ryan J. Stark argues, figurative language was never altogether absent from scientific writings by early Royal Society practitioners because the imagination was still considered to play an essential role in the making of scientific knowledge. Ryan J. Stark, *Rhetoric, Science, and Magic in Seventeenth-Century England* (Washington: The Catholic University of America Press, 2009), especially the introduction and chapter one.

be said to represent the misery of these times more lively to the reader,
or to give him a more perfect idea of a complicated distress? (p. 140)

In the exceptional scenario of a plague-infected city, there are sights
that challenge the observer's ability to describe them. H.F.'s use of
plain language acknowledges this challenge by choosing not to give
an interpretation to what he sees. The most significant episode of
H.F.'s voluntary aphasia is the visit to the mass grave. H.F. responds
to the invitation of the sexton to make sense of what he sees – ''twill
be a Sermon to you, it may be, the best that ever you heard in your
Life. 'Tis a speaking Sight [...] and has a Voice with it, and a loud
one, to call us all to Repentance' – with an aphasic comment which
rejects all possibilities of interpretation: 'it is impossible to say any
Thing that is able to give a true Idea of it to those who did not see it'.
H.F. opts for expressing the intensity of this frightening view not by
means of a metaphor but by the numerical accumulation of the same
basic adverb: 'it was indeed *very, very, very* dreadful, and such as no
Tongue can express' (p. 54).

This aphasia may be read as an application of the *hypotheses non
fingo*, one which is enforced by the fact that plague is 'impossible
to describe', a point H.F. reiterates on multiple occasions (e.g., pp.
69, 141). The plague, understood in the *Journal* as a manifestation
of nature that goes beyond the human intellect, teaches man that
human interpretation can only convey inaccurate ideas vitiated by
our use of the imagination. H.F.'s focus on the interferences of the
imagination – as expressed in his criticism of the mistaken beliefs
of lay people, the medical conjectures on the plague, the bills of
mortality, and the figurative language used to describe the plague
– makes the *Journal* a kind of meta-historical work, in that it aims
at interrogating the practices by which historical knowledge on
the 1665 plague came to be constructed and socially accepted. At
the same time, and in line with his *hypotheses non fingo* approach,
H.F. avoids claiming any degree of certainty for his statements,
even when they are just stories about Londoners during the Great
Plague, which are, at best, 'true in the general' (p. 47). While telling
the 'Story of the three Men', a moralizing narrative insert on three
people who attempted to escape from the plague, H.F. disclaims that

he will deliver the 'story' only if the reader refrains from asking him 'to either vouch the Particulars, or answer for any Mistakes'. Particulars cannot be verified, and H.F.'s argument that 'the History will be a very good Pattern for any poor Man to follow, in case the like public desolation should happen here', reveals the impossibility of committing to certainty even when it comes to storytelling. The reason is, once more, that 'it was impossible any particular Person cou'd come at the Knowledge of all the extraordinary Cases that occurr'd in different Families' (p. 131).

As with the other novels he published, in the *Journal* the epistemology of fact and fiction was a key concern for Defoe, particularly in terms of his reflection on the standards of historical truth-telling in extreme situations. Defoe, Alan McKinley claims, was 'acutely aware' that in the first decades of the eighteenth century 'the divide between fiction and fact, porous for so long, was hardening', and that there were new requirements in place for establishing facts.[84] The *Journal* thematizes a specific problem, that of what constitutes fact and fiction in a dire situation in which virtually nothing can be stated with certainty. Commentators have noted how in his novelistic output, and especially in *Robinson Crusoe*, Defoe attempted to 'rationalize' the use of fiction in the sense that he was 'careful not to outright say that his work is not factual'.[85] In the *Journal*, however, the focus is shifted to the criteria upon which one could determine the causes of a complex natural event and thus establish facts about it. Via his fictional narrator H.F., Defoe examines the problem of the epistemological validity of the imagination-based knowledge that circulates in a situation of crisis. H.F.'s chief occupation in his peregrinations as a chronicler of the plague-stricken London is that of reporting, and making sense of, the news surrounding the plague epidemics. He does so by debunking plague-related myths – including the medical theories that circulated to explain its causes – and raising the issue of whether a plague epidemic could be contained at all if one were to describe

---

84   Alan McKinlay, 'Foucault, Plague, Defoe', *Culture and Organization*, 15 (2009), 167–184 (p. 172).
85   Davis, Lennard, *Factual Fictions: The Origins of the English Novel* (Philadelphia: University of Pennsylvania Press, 1996), p. 156.

it accurately, all the while disclaiming that he was in no position of knowing anything with certainty.

In this way, Defoe revisits the problem of the fact-fiction divide via a compelling knowledge-making question. How does one make sense of a catastrophe like the Great Plague and offer an accurate description, given its being so difficult to describe compared to regular natural phenomena? In Newtonianist terms, Defoe's narrator H.F. criticises the faculty of imagination as the basis for plague-related knowledge, but the result he achieves is that no knowledge on plague can be made. In the extreme situation of a plague-stricken city, where the absence of reference points leads to a collective effort to imagine the nature of the disease, H.F. is the isolated subject who systematically challenges the body of imaginative assumptions and reports about pestilence. Paradoxically, the sole 'certainty of Things' that can be achieved in such a situation of epistemological crisis is that of admitting that nothing can be known for certain.

CHAPTER 4
SAGACIOUS DOUBT
Fielding's *Tom Jones* and the Problem of Deceitfulness

4.1. *Science and Fielding's Interest in Truth and Falsehood*

Drawing on a tradition that went back to Samuel Butler's *Hudibras* (1663–1678), Thomas Shadwell's *The Virtuoso* (1676) and Aphra Behn's *The Emperor of the Moon* (1687), Henry Fielding was no stranger to satirising science. In his works, the stereotypical *virtuoso* is lampooned for being so engrossed in his experiments that he loses touch with reality. In *A Journey from This World to the Next* (1743), a mock travelogue detailing a journey to the afterlife, the fictional bookseller writes that the work had been 'shown to the R—l Society', whose members remained unimpressed because 'there was nothing in it wonderful enough for them'.[1]

Tongue-in-cheek references to the credulity of early experimenters, for whom not even the netherworld was extraordinary enough, were common in the first half of the eighteenth century.[2] But this and other negative portraits of Royal Society early scientists in Fielding's production – such as that of the *Familiar Letters*, where experimenters are described as 'Corrupters of Taste' idly engaged in the discovery of 'the Oddities and Frolicks of Nature' – have cemented Fielding's status as one of the staunchest critics of experimental science.[3] Influential scholars like Bertrand Goldgar and Martin Battestin have suggested that Fielding's writing was characterised by a 'consistently satirical attitude' towards scientific endeavours, and that he denied

---

1   Henry Fielding, *Miscellanies*, 3 vols, ed. by Bertrand A. Goldgar and Hugh Amory (Oxford: Clarendon Press, 1997), II, 87.

2   Coppola, pp. 32–36.

3   Matthew Risling, 'Ants, Polyps, and Hanover Rats: Henry Fielding and Popular Science', *Philological Quarterly*, 95 (2016), 25–44 (p. 25).

the importance of any endeavours by Royal Society practitioners because they engaged in 'unnatural' philosophy.[4] The curiosity-driven methods of early Royal Society experimenters were mocked by Fielding because, according to Michael McKeon, they imposed 'on the credulity of the reader', spreading useless information while making no real scientific progress.[5]

Such claims, Matthew Risling explains, tend to overestimate the extent of Fielding's criticism of science.[6] When it comes to what he believed were long-lasting scientific achievements, Fielding readily recognized their importance and praised them unconditionally, often by opposition to the Royal Society virtuosos he caricatured. In the metatheatrical play *Pasquin* (1737), Royal Society members are once more poked fun at when, in the final play within the play, a messenger coming from a 'great society' brings to the Queen of Ignorance 'certain curiosities', containing 'A horse's tail, which has a hundred hairs / More than are usual in it; and a tooth / Of elephant full half an inch too long; / With turnpike–ticket like an ancient coin'.[7] If this lacklustre collection is a clear parody of the cabinets of curiosities enjoyed by many Royal Society practitioners, the epilogue of the play actually turns to a celebration of science. 'Can the whole world in science match our soil? / Have they a Locke, a Newton, or a Boyle?', one of the characters asks. This was by no means a sardonic remark, as it appears from the ensuing couplet, where Fielding extols the achievements of William Shakespeare and Ben Jonson, whom are described as far superior to any other self-appointed 'greatest genius' from abroad.[8]

---

4   Henry Fielding, *The Covent-Garden Journal and A Plan of the Universal Register-Office*, ed. by Bertrand A. Goldgar (Oxford: Oxford University Press, 1988), p. 157; Henry Fielding, *The Journal of a Voyage to Lisbon, Shamela, and Occasional Writings*, ed. Martin Battestin (Oxford: Oxford University Press, 2008), p. 573.

5   Michael McKeon, *The Origins of the English Novel, 1600–1740* (Baltimore: Johns Hopkins University Press, 1987), p. 383.

6   Risling, p. 27.

7   Henry Fielding, *Pasquin: A Dramatick Satire on the Times* (London: Ed. Cook, 1787), p. 61.

8   Fielding, *Pasquin*, p. 63.

Cases like that of *Pasquin* show that Fielding was familiar with Newton's popularity. Not that this is particularly surprising. As a writer of what J. P. Hunter calls 'occasional forms', Fielding drew heavily on public discussions, and his plays and novels are rich in references to present-day matters, not to speak of the many articles he wrote in his life for periodicals like *Covent-Garden Journal* (1752).[9] Science was part of Fielding's gamut of discussion topics, which is understandable considering that his writing career blossomed right in the middle of what Larry Stewart famously called 'the rise of public science' – that is, decades of acute public interest in all things scientific.[10] After settling back to London from the University of Leiden, Fielding embarked on a successful career as a playwright with the comedy *Love in Several Masques*, published in 1728. This was the year just after Newton's death, which started a period that Feingold, following Fontenelle, called 'apotheosis' – two decades of heightened cultural re-elaboration of both the ideas and the figure of Newton.[11] At this time, as the translation of Fontenelle's *Elogium* puts it with rhetorical flourish, Newton's philosophy 'hath been adopted throughout England, it prevails in the Royal Society, and in all the excellent performances which have come from thence'.[12] Even allowing for some exaggeration on Fontenelle's part, the years immediately after Newton's death did see a sustained effort, in print especially but also via public demonstrations, to popularise the complexities of *Principia* and *Opticks* and create a widespread image of Newton as a genius whose preternatural abilities allowed him to understand nature like nobody had done before.

Fielding too was receptive to this rhetoric, as it appears from a passage in his early novel *The History of the Life of the Late Mr. Jonathan Wild the Great* (1743), in which the narrator wonders at those ladies who still prefer a *beau* to Shakespeare, Milton, or Newton:

---

9   J. Paul Hunter, *Occasional Form: Henry Fielding and the Chains of Circumstance* (Baltimore: Johns Hopkins University Press, 1975).

10   Stewart; see also Coppola, pp. 180–186.

11   Feingold, *Newtonian Moment*, p. 170.

12   Fontenelle, pp. 25–26.

> For my own part, let any man chuse to himself two beaus, let them
> be captains or colonels, as well-dressed men as ever lived, I would
> venture to oppose a single Sir Isaac Newton, a Shakespear, a Milton,
> or perhaps some few others, to both these beaus; nay, and I very much
> doubt whether it had not been better for the world in general that neither
> of these beaus had ever been born than that it should have wanted the
> benefit arising to it from the labour of any one of those persons.[13]

As in the epilogue to *Pasquin*, the association with Shakespeare
and Milton suggests that Fielding recognized Newton as one of the
leading lights of the culture of his age, one that could be praised
regardless of specialist knowledge of his works. This characterisation
of Newton as a cultural icon also shares some similarities with
Henry Pemberton's *A View of Sir Isaac Newton's Philosophy*,
the most famous of the commentaries on Newton available when
Fielding began his career as a writer, and one which he owned.[14] If
in Pemberton's *View*, Newton is described in poetical terms as 'the
boast of this nation', Fielding muses on the injustice of a 'single
beau' being valued more, 'in the scale of female affection', than
'twenty Sir Isaac Newtons'.[15]

In light of this, the argument that Fielding's references to science
evince 'a solid grounding in popular science and the conventions
of scientific writing' might be extended to argue for a keen interest
in natural philosophy.[16] We know from Frederick Ribble and Anne
Ribble's annotated catalogue of his library that Fielding owned
works by Bacon, Boyle and Locke, as well as late-seventeenth-
century classics of natural philosophy such as Ralph Cudworth's
True Intellectual System (1678) and Richard Cumberland's *A Treatise
of the Laws of Nature* (1672). George Berkeley's *Siris* (1744),
and David Hume's *Enquiry Concerning Human Understanding*
(1748) were among his recent acquisitions, and the collection was
complemented by a selection of important philosophical works by

---

13   Fielding, *Miscellanies*, III, 101.
14   Frederick G. Ribble and Anne G. Ribble, *Fielding's Library: An Annotated
      Catalogue* (Charlottesville: University Press of Virginia, 1996), pp. xxvii.
15   Pemberton, 'Dedication'; Fielding, *Miscellanies*, III, 101.
16   Risling, p. 27.

continental philosophers, among which Montaigne, Pascal, Spinoza and Malebranche.[17]

This interest in natural philosophy testifies to Fielding's attraction to what Henry Knight Miller calls the 'rational and enlarging discourse' of science, which in Fielding's time was symbolized by Newton.[18] As argued in Chapter 1, Newton's efforts in natural philosophy were praised because of his ability to restrain his imagination, thus allowing him to detect natural phenomena in an accurate manner. While this ability was typically identified as 'reason', other commentators preferred to define it as penetrating sight, and Newton was accordingly praised for his 'wonderful Sagacity'.[19] The sight metaphor was a powerful one to describe Newton, who was characterised as the one who had seen better than anyone, as well as the one who had opened the eyes of his fellow Britons. 'I could never concur', wrote James Jurin in 1734, that:

> the Great Inventor of this method, and the Author or [*sic*] so many other wonderful discoveries, never knew or thought of what to us appears so plain and manifest; that he who gave us so much Light, was in the dark himself; that he who opened our Eyes, had no sight of his own. For my part I can never concur with you in thinking that I see farther, or go beyond Sir Isaac Newton.[20]

At a time when poets conceived of reason as a 'Newtonian Sun' which clears the sight from the obfuscation of fiction and allows the penetrating observer to see nature's inner workings, Fielding reflected on whether one could determine the universal characteristics of human nature scientifically.[21] Hints of the way

---

17   Ribble and Ribble, p. xxxi.

18   Henry Knight Miller, 'Henry Fielding's Satire on the Royal Society', *Studies in Philology*, 57 (1960), 72–86 (pp. 79–81).

19   William Derham, *Astro-Theology: or, a Demonstration of the Being and Attributes of God, from a Survey of the Heavens* (London: W. Innys, 1715), p. 154.

20   James Jurin, *Geometry No Friend to Infidelity: or, A Defence of Sir Isaac Newton and the British Mathematicians, in a Letter to the Author of the Analyst* (London: T. Cooper, 1734), p. 70.

21   Walter Harte, *An Essay on Reason* (London: Lawton Gulliver, 1735), p. 13. On Fielding and human nature, see Golden Morris, 'Public Context and

scientific thought informed Fielding's reflections on knowledge-making processes may be found in brief observations scattered across his fiction. For instance, in the dedication to *An Apology for the Life of Mrs. Shamela Andrews* (1741) – the famous parody of Richardson's *Pamela* (1740) – the narrator, after having praised his dedicatee, adds that: 'it only remains to pay my Acknowledgments to an Author, whose Stile I have exactly followed in this Life, it being the properest for Biography. The Reader, I believe, easily guesses, I mean *Euclid's Elements*; it was *Euclid* who taught me to write'.[22]

References like this point not just to Fielding's wide-ranging scientific reading, but to a keen interest in epistemology. As Everett Zimmerman contends, a common characteristic shared by Fielding's fictional narrators is that they constantly comment, overtly or covertly, on the processes whereby facts are established.[23] Many of Fielding's works are animated by the problem of distinguishing truth from falsehood, particularly in relation to the opposition between the true nature of a person and their appearances or words. Examples abound. The aforementioned *Jonathan Wild* is the story of a rogue who successfully becomes rich by manipulating his appearances, escaping justice by taking advantage of loopholes in the law of evidence and enjoying the favour of the crowd during his execution. In *The History of Tom Jones, a Foundling* (1749), which in the words of a commentator is best understood as a book about 'the understanding necessary for good judgment', the plot is set in motion by a twisted representation of the behaviour of the main character to Allworthy, who is both squire and Justice of the Peace.[24] In *Amelia* (1751), which begins with a string of unjust condemnations

---

Imagining Self in *Tom Jones*', *Papers on Language and Literature*, 20 (1984), 273–293.

22   Henry Fielding, *An Apology for the Life of Mrs. Shamela Andrews* (London: A. Dodd, 1741), 'Dedication'.

23   Zimmerman, p. 4. The third-person narrators in *Joseph Andrews*, *Tom Jones* and *Amelia*, Roger Maioli adds, always try to 'authenticate their narratives', either by claiming that a given event really happened or by emphasizing the probability that it could have happened. Roger Maioli, 'Empiricism and Henry Fielding's Theory of Fiction', *Eighteenth-Century Fiction*, 27 (2014), 201–228 (p. 217).

24   John Preston, '*Tom Jones* and the "Pursuit of True Judgment"', *ELH*, 33 (1966), 315–326 (p. 316).

by a corrupt judge emblematically named Mr. Thrasher, questions of truth-making are so central to the story that a scholar has identified links with the epistemology of the 'mechanical philosophy' of Boyle and Newton.[25]

At a close look, it appears that Fielding's scrutiny of the mechanics of truth-making was central to his overall intellectual outlook, not just to his fiction. The plot of one of his first plays, *Rape upon Rape* (1730), is based on the distortions about two alleged cases of sexual abuse by yet another corrupt judge. In *Shamela*, the frontispiece declares that the goal of the work is to correct the 'many notorious FALSEHOODS and MISREPRESENTATIONS' of Richardson's original, whose alleged fault is to have misunderstood Pamela's character.[26] The establishment of truth also proved to be a key concern to Fielding's legal experiences, first as a young lawyer and then, after his novelist career had ended, as a Justice of the Peace in Westminster. Because of his legal roles, Fielding was acutely aware of the challenges of passing judgment, especially whenever erroneous assessments would result in court decisions costing the life, or reputation, of innocent people.[27] This is what happened in 1749 with Bosavern Penlez, a twenty-three-year-old who was hanged because of a false testimony which Fielding, then a magistrate, had accepted as genuine. A similar situation occurred with the case of Elizabeth Canning, a maidservant who claimed to have been abducted. Fielding believed in her testimony, though it was never ascertained whether she had been honest or not. For both the Penlez and the Canning cases, Fielding would go on to write texts primarily devised to defend his decisions as a magistrate, but which doubled as reflections on how to find truth in specific circumstances.[28]

---

25   Glen Colburn, '"Struggling Manfully" through Henry Fielding's *Amelia*: Hysteria, Medicine, and the Novel in Eighteenth-Century England', *Studies in Eighteenth-Century Culture*, 26 (1997), 87–123 (p. 88).

26   Fielding, *Shamela*, 'Frontispiece'.

27   Martin C. Battestin and Ruthe R. Battestin, *Henry Fielding: A Life* (London and New York: Routledge, 1989), p. 462.

28   Henry Fielding, *A True State of the Case of Bosavern Penlez, who Suffered on Account of the Late Riot in the Strand* (London: A. Millar, 1749); Henry Fielding, *A Clear State of the Case of Elizabeth Canning Who Hath Sworn that She Was Robbed* (London: A. Millar, 1753).

In this chapter, it will be argued that Fielding's interest in the establishment of truth and falsehood was a reaction to the epistemological expectations set in place by Newtonianism, especially that the confidence in producing certain knowledge could be extended to the study of human nature. Before proceeding with this argument, it is first necessary to revisit the scholarly commonplace that reformation purposes were the driving reason for Fielding's reflections about truth and falsehood. This is the position embraced by Battestin in the influential Wesleyan edition of Fielding's three major novels (*Joseph Andrews*, *Tom Jones* and *Amelia*). In this view, Fielding's interest in truth-making is said to have resulted from his goal to promote social reform in favour of the destitute. In the biography Battestin wrote with Ruthe R. Battestin, Fielding is portrayed as he 'toil[s] in Covent Garden to dispense justice and help the poor', not unlike the Allworthy of *Tom Jones*. Errors of judgment are, like those of Allworthy, 'the consequence of an overweening confidence in his own perspicacity and the benevolence of his motives' which do not stain a magistracy defined as 'the story of an exemplary, even a sacrificial dedication to the public welfare'.[29] The primary aim of Fielding as described by the Battestins was educating fellow members of society to distinguish between good and evil. According to this line of interpretation, Fielding's goal was achieved by carefully weighing testimonies in the criminal court as well as by promoting examples of virtuous behaviours in his fiction.[30]

That the promotion of good nature and charity defined the ethical orientation of Fielding's entire work is a generous interpretation that conveniently overlooks Fielding's well-documented habit of lambasting the London poor in his newspapers, as well as his distinctly brutal record as a trial judge.[31] Scholars now understand

---

29   Battestin and Battestin, pp. 463, 468.

30   Martin C. Battestin, ed., *Twentieth Century Interpretations of Tom Jones* (Englewood Cliffs: Prentice-Hall, Inc., 1968), p. 10. See also Morris Golden, *Fielding's Moral Psychology* (Boston: The University of Massachusetts Press, 1966).

31   For Fielding's low opinion on the 'fourth estate', see the leader of the 47th issue of *Covent-Garden Journal* in Fielding, *Covent-Garden Journal*, pp. 259–264; Henry Fielding, *An Enquiry into the Causes of the Late Increase of*

Fielding's social and legal treatises written late in his life as being characterized by 'social and political conservatism', 'apparent acceptance of rigid class structures', and 'a willingness to deal with the poor and the underprivileged in ways that seem cruel'.[32] The main problem, however, is one of focus. As pointed out by Robert D. Hume, interpretations like that of the Battestins build mainly, if not exclusively, on the novels, without paying sufficient attention to the rest of the material published by Fielding, such as that in his role as social commentator.[33]

J. P. Hunter claimed that for Fielding, ethical practice was more relevant than epistemological abstractions.[34] As the rest of the chapter proceeds to show, this might be an oversimplification. Across his early essays, his fiction and his journal articles, Fielding tackled the question of whether it was possible to make knowledge about human nature with a degree of certainty akin to that of Newtonianism. He reached different answers depending on the medium he adopted. While in his philosophical writings sagacity is advocated as the ability to detect the principles regulating the behaviour of human nature, in the novel *Tom Jones* Fielding takes a more cautious position, suggesting that certainty in moral matters is something that can only be attained in fiction, and that only retrospectively.

Robbers and Related Writings, ed. by Malvin R. Zirker (Oxford: Clarendon Press, 1988), pp. xxii. Some scholars have convincingly argued that the textual apparatus of Battestin's Wesleyan edition of Fielding's novels shows a marked preference for quotations from English divines, as well as an unbalanced focus on the values of prudence and providence. See Ronald Paulson, '*The Jacobite's Journal and Related Writings by Henry Fielding*, W. B. Coley; *The History of Tom Jones: A Foundling* by Henry Fielding', *Modern Language Review*, 71 (1976), 888–891 (p. 891); Arthur Sherbo, 'Henry Fielding. *Joseph Andrews* by Martin C. Battestin', *Journal of English and Germanic Philology*, 67 (1968), 520–522 (p. 521).

32 Arlene Wilner, 'The Mythology of History, the Truth of Fiction: Henry Fielding and the Cases of Bosavern Penlez and Elizabeth Canning', *The Journal of Narrative Technique*, 21 (1991), 185–201 (p. 185).

33 Robert D. Hume, 'Fielding's *Plays* and the Completion of the Wesleyan Edition', *Huntington Library Quarterly*, 75 (2012), 447–463 (p. 452).

34 Hunter, pp. 3, 78, 80.

4.2. *The Ability of the Few: Sagacity in An Essay on the Knowledge of Character*

Included in the first volume of the 1743 *Miscellanies*, but probably written in the mid-1730s, the *Essay on the Knowledge of the Characters of Men* is a work in which Fielding examines the question of how to determine the true character of a person. With a fitting definition, the *Essay* has been defined as 'a handbook on hypocrisy', one possibly stemmed from Fielding's 'indignation at the fact that so many men have devoted themselves to inventing systems by which the cunning and unscrupulous might impose upon the rest of the world'.[35] This belief is exemplified by the beginning of the *Essay*:

> I have often thought it a melancholy instance of the great depravity of human nature, that, whilst so many men have employed their utmost abilities to invent systems, by which the artful and cunning part of mankind may be enabled to impose on the rest of the world, few or none should have stood up the champions of the innocent and undesigning, and have endeavoured to arm them against imposition.[36]

After this premise, Fielding sets out to discuss how the real personality of a person may be identified. This is done primarily by looking at three features: physiognomy, one's behaviour toward themselves, and one's behaviour toward other people.[37] The rules that Fielding tries to establish are somewhat self-contradictory – as a commentator puts it, the 'stance of the stern moralist' is constantly alternated with that of the 'well-intentioned but by no means omniscient guide'.[38] Fielding's descriptions of physical expressions in the section on physiognomy can indeed get quite convoluted. A 'constant, settled, glavering, sneering smile', for instance, is

---

35   Henry Knight Miller, *Essays on Fielding's* Miscellanies: *A Commentary on Volume One* (Princeton: Princeton University Press, 1961), p. 191.

36   Fielding, *Miscellanies,* I, 156. The next quotations will be cited parenthetically in the body of the text.

37   Arlene Wilner, 'Henry Fielding and the Knowledge of Character', *Modern Language Studies*, 18 (1988), 181–194 (p. 186).

38   Ibid.

indicative of evil-doing, but it is not to be confused with an 'amiable, open, composed, cheerful aspect', nor with a 'honest, hearty, loud chuckle', both of which are supposed to be signs of goodness (p. 156). A number of caveats also apply; for one, Fielding's analysis of laughter does not include 'the various laughs, titters, tehes' of the 'fair sex', as the characters of women 'is in fact a science to which I make not the least pretension' (p. 157).

Regardless of his success, from an epistemological perspective Fielding's claim that one can identify the real character of a person is a noteworthy endeavour because it is based on the adamantine conviction that the principles regulating human behaviour can be discovered via painstaking observation, much in the same way as natural phenomena may be discovered by the scrutinizing gaze of the philosopher. The foundations for this position are laid through an attack against those writers who, according to Fielding, would 'invent systems' to discover the principles that govern the behaviour on 'man in general' (p. 157). The critique of the invention of systems was a classical locus of natural philosophy commentaries in mid-eighteenth-century England, and the favourite target was Descartes, who, as a newspaper article would put it a few decades later, reprising a stereotypical argument, 'had recourse to constructing systems, which are merely the offspring of invention, and, like bubbles, vanish into air, when examined by the touchstone of true philosophy', i.e., Newton's.[39] Accordingly, at the beginning of the *Essay* an attack is waged at those who attempt to find uniformity in human nature. Such people, Fielding claims, seem 'not sufficiently to have studied human nature', and thus fail to notice the 'immense variety of characters' that make persons different from one another (p. 158).

In a surprising twist, a few pages later Fielding explains that humankind does have universal properties, chief of which is that of seeking the society of other people. Fielding's claim echoes an argument made some decades prior by George Berkeley, in which the classical Aristotelian dictum that man is a social animal was

---

39   *Lloyd's Evening Post and British Chronicle*, April 17, 1761 – April 20, 1761; Issue 578.

rehashed by linking it to Newton's scientific discoveries and made into a universal moral principle. Writing in 1713 in the *Guardian*, a short-lived periodical ran by Richard Steele, Berkeley maintained that a 'like principle of attraction operates in the Spirits or Minds of men [...] whereby they are drawn together in communities, clubs, families, friendships, and all the various species of society'.[40] This argument is elevated by Berkeley to the rank of a law of nature that has the same certainty of the gravitational force in the solar system identified by Newton. As Harry Elmer Barnes explains, Berkeley worked by analogy: as 'the attractive principle of the universe is the key to the natural phenomenon, so is the social instinct the source and explanation of all the various actions of man in society which may be called moral'.[41]

There is no clear evidence as to whether Fielding was familiar with Berkeley's argument in the *Guardian*, although this is not unlikely given that traces of Berkeley's *Siris* may be found in Fielding's later *The Journal of a Voyage to Lisbon*.[42] Nonetheless, Fielding too maintains that human sociability is one of the 'general rules of morality' that holds universally because it is constitutive of human nature (p. 160). In the *Essay on Conversation* (1743), which was written at about the same time as the *Essay on Characters* and was also included in the *Miscellanies*, Fielding reiterates that there is indeed a 'general rule' of man 'being a social animal', and then proceeds to make use of this general rule to mount arguments on what proper conversation is – an argument which, as Fielding explains with reference to a traditional natural philosophy image, will be found true by 'whoever is well read in the book of nature'.[43]

---

40   George Berkeley, *Works*, 9 vols, ed. by A. A. Luce and T. E. Jessop (London: T. Nelson, 1948–57), VII, 225–228. See also A. A. Luce, 'Berkeley's Essays in the *Guardian*', *Mind*, 52 (1943), 247–263.

41   Harry Elmer Barnes, 'Bishop Berkeley's Essay on Moral Attraction: An Illustration of the Influence of Seventeenth Century Natural Science on Social Philosophy', *The Open Court*, 4 (1922), 251–256 (p. 253)

42   Richard Gooding, '"A Complication of Disorders": Bodily Health, Masculinity, and the Discourse of Gout and Dropsy in Henry Fielding's *The Journal of a Voyage to Lisbon*', *Literature and Medicine*, 26 (2007), 386–407.

43   Henry Fielding, *Miscellanies*, I, 130.

It is not immediately easy to reconcile Fielding's claim for universal human properties with that on human nature displaying immense variety in its manifestations. While this could be a typical instance of what Empson calls Fielding's 'double irony' – his ability to hold two positions at odds with each other – it is the use of sagacity which provides a bridge between the variety of particular manifestations and the presence of universal patterns.[44] As Deidre Lynch contends, literate men in eighteenth-century Britain fashioned themselves as 'the beneficiaries of a symbolic environment that was founded on principles of perspicuity and accessibility and in which truths could be self-evident'. To people with a certain degree of literacy, even new events for which no past experience was available could still be interpreted with the assuredness reserved to the discovery of scientific facts, because they had epistemic protocols in place which ensured comparability between known and unknown phenomena.[45]

In a similar way, Fielding suggests that the dazzling variety of manifestations in people's character may be made sense of by sagacious penetration. The variety of human behaviour, he argues, is deceitful only if what is shown is accepted as true at face value. To the eye of the 'accurate observer', by contrast, face value is irrelevant, for nature is 'ever endeavouring to peep forth and show herself' from behind disguises:

> [H]owever cunning the disguise be which a masquerade wears; however foreign to his age, degree, or circumstance, yet if closely attended to, he very rarely escapes the discovery of an accurate observer; for Nature, which unwillingly submits to the imposture, is ever endeavouring to peep forth and show herself; [...] In the same manner will those disguises, which are worn on the greater stage, generally vanish, or prove ineffectual to impose the assumed for the real character upon us, if we employ sufficient diligence and attention in the scrutiny. (p. 156)

---

44   William Empson, 'Tom Jones', *Kenyon Review*, 20 (1958), 27–49 (p. 32).

45   Deidre Lynch, *The Economy of Character: Novels, Market Culture, and the Business of Inner Meaning* (Chicago and London: Chicago University Press, 1998), p. 5.

In the *Essay*, Fielding establishes an opposition between the voice of nature and knowledge produced by people. His scepticism is directed towards those who rely on personal testimony as the gauge of the real character of a person. As Fielding clarifies, there is no 'more simple, unjust, and insufficient Method of judging Mankind, than by public estimation', and 'the Few Rules which generally prevail' in this respect are 'utterly false, and the very Reverse of Truth', given that we 'almost universally mistake the Symptoms which Nature kindly holds forth to us' (pp. 156–157).

The 'diligence and attention in the scrutiny' which are required to understand real human characters beyond appearances are limited to the few who recognize that man is structurally prone to distort what he sees. Only philosophical-inclined people are able to look at the 'Actions of Men', which for Fielding are the 'surest Evidence of their Character', rather than their appearances. This ability depends on making use of 'an accurate and discerning Eye', which is 'the Property of the few', while 'the Generality of Mankind mistake the Affectation for the Reality' (p. 162).

For those few gifted individuals who can mistrust their prejudices, Fielding enumerates 'the principal Methods by which Deceit works its Ends on easy, credulous, and open Disposition' (p. 162). Accordingly, in this final part of the *Essay* Fielding re-configures his intervention as a 'Guide to direct us to the Knowledge of Men' – a guide on the effectiveness of which 'we may with the greatest Certainty rely' because it is based on Fielding's own discerning observation (p. 174). While the 'certainty' about men and their characters claimed by Fielding is not explicitly likened to that of mathematics – the adjective 'greatest' is a linguistic choice that conveys certainty by degrees rather than absolutes – Fielding does suggest that his ability to assess the actions of men rather than their speech or appearances leads to an increase of the degree of probability so high that it attains the rank of nigh certainty. In response to a possible question on 'how shall we then distinguish with any Certainty the true from the fictitious?', Fielding responds that with sagacity a fact is established through a ratio of 'Ninety Nine Times in a Hundred' (p. 168) – that is, almost completely certain. In other words, Fielding claims that the true character of a person may be determined with certainty in spite of all misleading fictional appearances, as long as the observer is sagacious enough.

4.3. *Deceitfulness and Conjectures in Tom Jones*

The belief, presented by Fielding in the *Essay on Characters*, that humankind is generally unable to tell truth from fiction finds its thematization in *The History of Tom Jones, a Foundling*, a story which, as the reader is repeatedly told, is about 'human nature' (a keyword used three times in the opening chapter alone).[46] Deception is a key concept in the novel, as it appears from the moment the titular character is finally introduced in Book 3 of 24. Pledging to follow the 'Directions of Truth', the narrator introduces Tom Jones by claiming that:

> As we determined, when we first sat down to write this history, to flatter no man, but to guide our pen throughout by the directions of truth, we are obliged to bring our hero on the stage in a much more disadvantageous manner than we could wish; and to declare honestly, even at his first appearance, that it was the universal opinion of all Mr Allworthy's family that he was certainly born to be hanged.
>
> Indeed, I am sorry to say, there was too much Reason for this Conjecture. (p. 109)

The rationale for the conjecture which characterises Tom Jones lies in what the narrator calls the 'vices of this young man' – in fact, venial juvenile mistakes which, artfully magnified by Tom Jones's step-brother Blifil, cast him in a negative light with his adoptive father Allworthy, resulting in his being unjustly dismissed from the squire's home.

Critics have noted how such an introduction plays with the conventions of the early novel, playfully linking Tom Jones's unruly behaviour as a young boy to criminal biographies which, like

---

46 Henry Fielding, *The History of Tom Jones, a Foundling*, ed. by Thomas Keymer and Alice Wakely (London: Penguin Books, 1974), pp. 35–37. Next references to the text in parentheses.

Jonathan Wild, end up with the main character being imprisoned or executed.[47] What deserves further scrutiny, however, are the epistemological ramifications of this presentation, which is replete with the scientifically-charged vocabulary of 'universal Opinion', 'Conjecture' and 'Reason'. This language characterizes Tom Jones's supposed moral depravity as a very reasonable conjecture – one so well-founded that its validity is shared 'universally', but a conjecture nonetheless. In fact, as readers discover at the end of the novel, this conjecture was wrong all along, even though it was believed to be valid by most characters in the story. Far from being hanged, the plot culminates with a vindication of the reputation of Jones and the access to his rightful estate as the nephew of Allworthy. This final twist is a reversal of the conventional aristocratic concept of honour – the main character, who appeared to everyone like a felon, is revealed to be an aristocrat – but also a challenge to interpretive expectations, for the reader too is made to fall for this erroneous, yet plausible conjecture.[48] As Homer O. Brown has shrewdly remarked, the very title of the novel, with its reference to Tom Jones being a foundling, is misleading in light of the final developments in the plot, and is evidently meant to trigger some confusion on the part of the reader.[49]

With this introduction, a tension is thus instated between the knowledge available to the characters within the novel and that which is reserved to the narrator. The principle, explored in the *Essay on Characters*, that the few endowed with penetration are able to see the discrepancy between the 'actions of men' and their words and appearances finds its case study in *Tom Jones,* where, using narrative as 'a laboratory for controlled observation' (in the words of John Bender), Fielding designs highly-rational characters who, however,

---

47   Martin A. Kayman, 'The "New Sort of Specialty" and the "New Province of Writing": Bank Notes, Fiction and the Law in *Tom Jones*', *ELH*, 68 (2001), 633–653 (p. 634).

48   Terence N. Bowers, 'Fielding's *Odyssey*: The Man of Honor, the New Man, and the Problem of Violence in Tom Jones', *Studies in Philology*, 115 (2018), 803–834 (p. 804).

49   See Homer O. Brown, 'Tom Jones: The "Bastard" of History', *boundary2*, 7 (1979), 201–33 (p. 201).

cannot help being deceived.[50] The most significant instance is that of Allworthy, who throughout the novel is repeatedly depicted not only as a paragon of moral rectitude (as implied by the name), but also as the epitome of rationality. A justice of peace in his squiredom, Allworthy is endowed with an acute sense of 'the first Principles of natural Justice' (p. 76) and an instinctive understanding of the dictates of the 'Law of Nature' (p. 88). And yet, not even he is able to avoid being deceived, and casts Jones away from his house after a stratagem from Jones's stepbrother Blifil. Lest the reader supposes that Allworthy is at fault for his misjudgement, Jones himself, at the end of the story, clarifies that this was not the case. Even the wisest person, Jones tells Allworthy, 'might be deceived as you were, and, under such Deception, the best must have acted as you did' (p. 853). Readers can therefore trust Allworthy's good faith when, looking back at his drastic decision to send Jones away from his estate, he concludes that 'it was upon the fullest and plainest Evidence that I resolved to take the Measures I have taken' (p. 799).

The problem of misinterpretation lies not in one's intentions but in a structural impossibility of seeing through deception, even for such a pinnacle of rationality as Allworthy. It is the flawed nature of humankind which is responsible for the error committed by Allworthy, who would have needed super-human knowledge – 'the Insight of the Devil', as the narrator calls it – to have 'entertained the least Suspicion of what was going forward' (p. 66). In fact, as Nicholas Hudson highlights, in Fielding's narratives characters are systematically subject to 'failures of discernment'. Parson Adams in *Joseph Andrews*, Heartfree in *Jonathan Wild*, Allworthy in *Tom Jones*, and Booth and Amelia in *Amelia* end up suffering because of their inability to see through deception, which, in Fielding's narrative worlds, is the 'primary source of danger'.[51]

In *Tom Jones*, the character of Allworthy serves as an example of the philosophical argument that humans are prone to be deceived.

50 John Bender, *Imagining the Penitentiary: Fiction and the Architecture of Mind in Eighteenth-Century England* (Chicago: Chicago University Press, 1989), pp. 183–184.

51 Nicholas Hudson, 'Fielding and the "Sagacious Reader": A Response to Lothar Černy', *Connotations*, 3 (1993), 79–84 (p. 80).

Supporting evidence of this view comes through general statements on human behaviour uttered by different characters in the occasional moments when they reassess the events in the plot. For example, as Sophia (Jones's lover and, finally, spouse) puts it at the very end of the novel, with a philosophical accent that is reminiscent of the language used by Fielding in the *Essay on Characters*, the 'human Mind may be imposed on; nor is there any infallible Method to prevent it' (p. 866).

Conversely, other episodes in *Tom Jones* show that it is also part of human nature not to tell the whole truth on a given matter, or to tell it in such a way as to receive an advantage. Jones seems to accept his being wrongly condemned on the philosophical grounds that 'Appearances […] are often deceitful' and that 'Men sometimes look like what they are not' (p. 394). Jones himself is unable to evaluate the veracity of other people's speech or appearances. One of his chief characteristics, the narrator notes, is a 'blameable Want of Caution and Diffidence in the Veracity of others' (p. 376). At the same time, Jones is described as having 'the most deceitful Countenance' (p. 381), which leads him, like everyone else, to seek advantage from the stories he tells. As the narrator explains to the reader in one of the meta-textual inserts that punctuate the text:

> let a Man be never so honest, the Account of his own Conduct will, in Spite of himself, be so very favourable, that his Vices will come purified through his Lips […] so different will be the Motives, Circumstances, and Consequences, when a Man tells his own Story, and when his Enemy tells it, that we scarce can recognize the Facts to be one and the same. (p. 370)

The resulting principle – which might be formulated as 'humans are naturally prone to both deceive and be deceived' – regulates virtually all the events in *Tom Jones*. In fact, the plot unfolds due to the characters' overall inability to see what lies behind other people's appearances. While characters seem to be lost in a mire of deception, however, Fielding's reader sits in a privileged, detached position from which to observe the actions of the characters unfold under the tutelage of the narrator. As in the example above, the past tense narrative of the events in *Tom Jones* is often frozen so that the narrator can engage directly in a conversation with the reader, delivering observations in the present tense, which, as signalled by the shift in verb tense, are presented as general truths about human behaviour. For example, commenting on Blifil's promise to Mr. Dowling, the lawyer hired to destroy evidence of Jones's blood relation to Allworthy, the narrator pithily states that '[i]t is possible for Man to convey a lie in the words of truth' (p. 844).

This tense shift is significant. The use of the present tense, as Peter Dear has shown, characterised mathematical texts in the long eighteenth century. This grammatical choice signified that mathematical demonstrations are always true irrespective of the context. This mode stood in opposition to experiment narratives, which, being accounts of a specific moment in time, tended to be told in the past tense to buttress their authenticity.[52] Similarly, in *Tom Jones* Fielding interrupts his tale at specific moments to state universal truths from the story, as if he was deriving general laws from the data contained in the story. In this way, the narrator of *Tom Jones* can fashion himself as the accurate observer of human nature described in the *Essay*, one who is able to read through deception and identify the universal principles that regulate the behaviour of humankind. Not unlike the Newton described in newspapers in these years, the narrator of *Tom Jones* presents himself as able to guide the reader through 'the intricate mazes of hypothesis and conjecture', making 'Nature [appear] again, in all her primitive simplicity'.[53] In effect, in *Tom Jones* the narrator claims that he had drawn 'his Materials from Nature only' (p. 931), a tendency which is accompanied by disdain for knowledge obtained through textual sources:

> For however exquisitely human Nature may have been described by Writers, the true practical System can be learnt only in the World. Indeed the like happens in every other Kind of Knowledge. Neither Physic, nor Law, are to be practically known from Books. (p. 997)

---

52   Peter Dear, *Discipline and Experience: The Mathematical Way in the Scientific Revolution* (Chicago: Chicago University Press, 1995), p. 201.

53   *Adventurer*, Tuesday, March 5, 1754; Issue 139.

Playing the part of the natural philosopher, the narrator shows that none of the characters in *Tom Jones* are endowed with the sagacity that would allow them to see through deception, but that he, as a narrator, is indeed sagacious.

Readers are invited to learn from the narrator's penetrating sight and turn philosophers themselves. The sagacity which Fielding advocates for his readers is not meant as the physician's skill of 'finding out and using signs' which, according to Douglas Lane Patey, provided Fielding 'with a paradigm of the processes of judgment by which we come to know [a] character and penetrate the meaning of events'.[54] The sagacity in question is the more philosophical one defined by William Sharpe in 1755 as the ability of detecting universal truths, 'a quicksightedness into men and things' and a 'penetration into moral or scientific truth'.[55] In this sense, what Fielding demands from his readers is that they interest themselves in the epistemology of how the plot unravels, rather than just the plot itself.[56] This type of guided textual enlightenment, however, is not to be used to cast judgment on the mistaken decisions taken by characters in the novel. Even though Allworthy is wrong in his judgments, the narrator warns those who 'condemn the Wisdom or Penetration of Mr. Allworthy' that 'they make a very bad and ungrateful Use of that Knowledge which we have communicated to them' (p. 123). The narrator's addresses to the reading audience are part of a pedagogy by which the latter are instructed to be aware of the complexities of knowledge-making, but what is being taught seems to be less that the reader should learn 'to tolerate the alternation between doubt and affirmation of one's reality, suspending judgment and passing judgment, and relaxing and asserting control', as has been noted by Susan McNamara, than that judgment should be suspended altogether, given that anybody

---

54   Douglas Lane Patey, *Probability and the Literary Form: Philosophic Theory and Literary Practice in the Augustan Age* (Cambridge: Cambridge University Press, 1984), pp. 62, 208.

55   William Sharpe, *A Dissertation upon Genius; Or, an Attempt to Shew, That the Several Instances of Distinction, and Degrees of Superiority in the Human Genius are not, fundamentally, the Result of Nature, but the Effect of Acquisition* (London: C. Bathurst, 1755) p. 56.

56   Sandra Sherman, 'Reading at Arm's Length: Fielding's Contract with the Reader in *Tom Jones*', *Studies in the Novel*, 30 (1998), 232–245 (p. 238).

in the position of the characters in *Tom Jones* would have made the same mistakes.[57]

Given that Fielding does not pursue moral condemnation on the part of his readers, what he expects is a reflection on the deep epistemological grounds which underlie the mistakes in judgment made by as reasonable a person as Allworthy. This interpretive key is provided by the narrator himself when, in one of his philosophical intermezzos, he states that:

> it is our Business to relate Facts as they are; which when we have done, it is the Part of the learned and sagacious Reader to consult that original Book of Nature, whence every Passage in our Work is transcribed, tho' we quote not always the particular Page for its Authority. (p. 335)

With the privilege of distance from the story being told, the duty of the 'learned and sagacious Reader' is not to evaluate the particulars of the plot, but to 'consult that original Book of Nature' to verify, and confirm, the principles that cause even somebody as reasonable as Allworthy to be mistaken about human nature. As Malinda Snow puts it, what readers learn in *Tom Jones* is not so much to judge better, but to be more cautious in their judgments.[58] In this respect, *Tom Jones* is a novel in which readers are expected to become sceptical observers of human behaviour.

4.4. *Lacking Sagacity: Fielding's Critique of Natural Philosophy*

Examining his fiction from the angle of emotional excess, Glen Colburn has observed that Fielding 'advocates an inductive methodology' for the examination of human behaviour.[59] This methodology, which Colburn argues to be influenced by the work

---

57 Susan P. McNamara, 'Mirrors of Fiction Within *Tom Jones*: The Paradox of Self-Reference', *Eighteenth-Century Studies*, 12 (1979), 372–390 (p. 374).

58 Malinda Snow, 'The Judgment of Evidence in *Tom Jones*', *South Atlantic Review*, 48 (1983), 37–51 (p. 37). On the question of law in *Tom Jones*, see also Carl R. Kropf, 'Judgment and Character, Evidence and the Law in "Tom Jones"', *Studies in the Novel*, 21 (1989), 357–366.

59 Colburn, p. 88.

of iatro-mechanical physicians like George Cheyne and Thomas Sydenham, requires that 'Fortune' (and thus wonder) be discarded as an explanation for 'ordinary Phenomena', opting instead for explanations based on the careful observation of 'natural Means'. A formulation was offered in the first chapter of *Amelia*, Fielding's final novel published two years after *Tom Jones*:

> By examining carefully the several gradations which conduce to bring every Model to Perfection, we learn truly to know that Science in which the Model is formed: As Histories of this Kind, therefore, may properly be called Models of Human Life; so by observing minutely the several Incidents which tend to the Catastrophe or Completion of the whole, and the minute Causes whence those Incidents are produced, we shall best be instructed in this most useful of all Arts, which I call the Art of Life.[60]

In light of this ambition to deduce moral phenomena scientifically via a minute observation of human dealings, 'sagacity' in Fielding's novels, and particularly in *Tom Jones*, may be understood as the quality needed to achieve this goal. As Henry Power has reconstructed, Fielding employs the words 'sagacious', 'sagacity' and 'sagaciousness' 41 times across *Tom Jones*, and all of them in addresses to the reader, with none of the characters being defined in these terms.[61] This data shows Fielding's confidence that sagacity may be transposed from fiction into reality – that is, that readers may be made into 'sagacious' observers even beyond the boundaries of the novel. The lack of wonderful events and the interest in verisimilitude in *Tom Jones* – what Goldgar has called Fielding's 'outright preference' for fact over fiction – reinforces the idea that in Fielding's narratological outlook there is a continuity between the textual reality of the novel and the extra-textual one of the readers.[62] As Wolfgang Iser put it when he applied his familiar reader response argument to *Tom Jones*, the 'repertoire of the familiar' gets

---

60 Ibid.
61 Henry Power, 'Henry Fielding, Richard Bentley, and the "Sagacious Reader" of *Tom Jones*', *The Review of English Studies*, 61 (2010), 749–772 (p. 750).
62 Bertrand A. Goldgar, 'Fielding on Fiction and History', *Eighteenth-Century Fiction*, 7 (1995), 279–292 (p. 279).

reproduced in Fielding's novel with slight modifications, which impels the reader to seek what Iser calls 'positive potential' – that is, 'the alternate fulfilment of [...] the realization of the text'.[63]

This pragmatic value inherent in *Tom Jones*, as Stephen Dobranski has astutely observed, does not apply to all readers, but only to a special class which are identified by the narrator as those 'who are admitted behind the Scenes of this great Theatre of Nature'. Such readers are able to become sagacious as long as they are 'thoroughly acquainted not only with the several Disguises which are there put on, but also with the fantastic and capricious Behaviour of the Passions who are the Managers and Directors of this Theatre'.[64] In other words, this select group of sagacious readers are invited to partake in Fielding's philosophical belief that universal truths about human behaviour can indeed be determined with certainty, notwithstanding misleading appearances.

What is unclear, however, is the extent to which the reader should trust Fielding's voice, if anything because, by Fielding's own sceptical reasoning, his being a human observer makes him as subject to deceive and being deceived as anyone else. Fielding himself was conscious of this conundrum, and strategically has his narrator in *Tom Jones* disclaim that, notwithstanding his universal claims on the nature of humankind scattered throughout the text, he is not 'writing a System, but a History, and I am not obliged to reconcile every Matter to the received Notions concerning Truth and Nature' (p. 573). But accepting this disclaimer significantly dilutes Fielding's pretension to being able to scientifically determine human nature that he had presented in the *Essay on Characters*. Crucially, Fielding's admission makes for a serious limitation in his advocacy of sagacity, because it compromises the possibility that such an ability applies to the empirical world.

This final realization is at the core of a piece on natural philosophy that appeared in *The Covent-Garden Journal* in 1752, a short-lived

---

63   Wolfgang Iser, *The Implied Reader: Patterns of Communication in Prose Fiction from Bunyan to Beckett* (Baltimore: Johns Hopkins University Press, 1974), pp. 34–35.

64   Stephen B. Dobranski, 'What Fielding Doesn't Say in *Tom Jones*', *Modern Philology*, 107 (2010), 632–653 (p. 648).

periodical Fielding edited after he had published his final novel *Amelia* in 1751, and while engaged with his activity as a Justice of Peace in Westminster. Reviewing *An Account of English Ants* written in 1747 by William Gould, an entomologist and Fellow of the Royal Society, Fielding's mouthpiece Sir Alexander Drawcansir agrees with the author that 'some moral lessons for the use of mankind' could be drawn from the study of ants.[65] From thence, Drawcansir embarks on a meditation on the similarities between these insects and humans. One of the chief qualities of ants is their 'sagacity', and Drawcansir speculates that 'these little insects may possibly resemble the human species', specifically in their having developed sciences that, like ours, 'end in nothing, and produce no effect at all'. This criticism of the sciences references 'the higher branches of natural philosophy' as a particularly useless field of knowledge. Reversing Fontenelle's famous advice that '[w]hen we are for prying into Nature we ought to examine her like Sir Isaac', Drawcansir mounts a satirical attack against natural philosophers because of their tendency to be 'always prying into the secrets of nature':

> Such for instance among us are the higher branches of natural philosophy; that philosophy, I mean, which is always prying into the secrets of nature, and lying in wait as it were to peep into her dressing-room to view her naked, and before she is drest in any kind of form. A bold attempt, and for which the philosophers have been often deprived of that little share of sense which they before possessed. Indeed, I am apt to think, that if a superior being was to examine into the ways of man [...] he would not be able to make any thing of this philosopher, nor to discover what he was about when he was employed in his lucubrations.[66]

At this point, the *Covent-Garden Journal* piece transitions to a dreamy speculation. As Drawcansir dozes off, he dreams of an assembly of insect natural philosophers. In an obvious parody of Royal Society meetings, 'one of the Insects, that was elevated above the rest on a small Bit of Earth [...] seemed to address himself to the

---

65   *The Covent-Garden Journal*, Saturday, November 11, 1752; Issue 70.
66   Ibid.

rest in the following Speech'.[67] This was evidently the president of the Royal Society, who talks to the assembly about the importance of their endeavours, and their achievements so far:

> Now by what can we hope to effect this so certainly, as by that Investigation of Nature, that Search into the first Causes of things, which as it is the noblest and most useful of all Studies, so is it most fitly accommodated to the Dignity of an Ant, the noblest Insect which this World ever saw.[68]

This scathing mockery of the confidence of natural philosophers makes one wonder if the ant philosopher 'elevated above the rest' is Newton, with whom the investigation of nature and into the first causes of things was associated, and who had run the Royal Society for twenty-five years, from 1703 to his death in 1727. The reference to the lexicon of certainty, to the search into first causes, and the dismissal of a competing theory by 'that mighty Ant, Dr. Hook', is suggestive, if inconclusive, evidence in this regard.[69]

Regardless of whether it was Newton in particular who Fielding had in mind, what is striking in this vignette depicting a community of ant natural philosophers are the epistemological implications. Not only are the achievements of natural philosophers belittled by their being likened to ants. Fielding's piece also suggests that only in fictional, dream-like worlds, where humankind is symbolically rendered as minuscule 'ant-kind', is it possible to conduct 'that investigation of nature, that search into the first causes of things' which is 'the noblest and most useful of all studies'. The degree of certainty and perfection that Newtonianist commentators argued was within human grasp if only a Newton-like sagacity was exercised, is here considered by Fielding as an absurd, chimerical enterprise beyond the ability of man.

This represented a dramatic about face from the philosophical confidence Fielding himself had displayed in the *Essay on Characters*. Whether the change was due to the fact that, as John

---

67   Ibid.
68   Ibid.
69   Ibid.

Bender suggests, Fielding 'wore himself out as justice of the piece, pamphleteer, and proponent of legislation', thus relinquishing all philosophical ambitions, is a fascinating speculation.[70] It is more likely, however, that in the two-fold transition from philosophical reflection to fiction and to fiction to legal judgment, Fielding had to come to terms with the 'epistemological uncertainty' that resulted from what Wilner defines a conflict between 'belief and experience'.[71]

Novels are the heuristic devices by which Fielding explored his 'epistemological concerns', and, specifically, 'the ways in which both characters in novels and readers of novels attempt to organize discrete perceptions into constructed paradigms'.[72] In the fictional mechanism created in *Tom Jones*, Fielding makes use of the privilege of narrative omniscience, oscillating between what John Warner calls 'an inductive and a deductive view of experience', to essentially suggest his readers that, if they have sagacity enough, they will be able to reconcile their observations to their general ideas about human behaviour.[73] But this confidence is actually undermined by the fact that the only knowledge the reader can take away from reading a novel like *Tom Jones* is that as humans we are bound to fail because we tend to trust appearances and fall prey to deception. As Leona Toker has put it, Fielding's readers are faced 'with a series of challenges to our sagacity and moral judgment':

> The mystification is among the challenges: it tests our sagacity—but the test is 'fixed', and we cannot help failing. We may well know that 'to err is human', yet we learn it all over again through a personal, non-vicarious experience in which vexation and its compensation can hardly be distinguished.[74]

---

70 Bender, *Imagining the* Penitentiary, p. 184.
71 Wilner, 'Mythology of History', p. 187.
72 Wilner, 'Mythology of History', p. 188.
73 John M. Warner, 'The Interpolated Narratives in the Fiction of Fielding and Smollett: An Epistemological View', *Studies in the Novel*, 5 (1973), 271–283 (p. 272).
74 Leona Toker, *Eloquent Reticence: Withholding Information in Fictional Narrative* (Lexington, KY: University Press of Kentucky, 1993), p. 106.

The contradictory stance on sagacity in *Tom Jones* points to the possibility that what Thomas Lockwood calls Fielding's 'capacity to transform matter into reflection' is one that may be only achieved under the specific conditions provided by fictional distance.[75] Readers are indeed expected to become sagacious, but it is unclear whether they can actually do so outside of fiction.

In this regard, a novel like *Tom Jones* predates the criticism to natural philosophy Fielding would level in the *Covent-Garden Journal* piece, insofar as his contemporary readers, like the ant natural philosophers, are stuck in a 'comic gulf' between their grand assumption that they could identify the principles of human nature, and the harsh 'existential reality' that they are unable to see through deception.[76] If the tension between the 'rage for order and the senseless brutality of fact' which transpires from Fielding's *Tom Jones* belies, and frustrates, the philosophical endeavour to detect the ideals of human nature and make them into a science, this does not mean that Fielding completely reneges the methods of natural philosophy.[77] Rather, what Fielding offers is a sobering counterpoint to the Newtonianist confidence in the knowledge-making capabilities of humankind, creating for his readers what Leo Braudy calls an 'atmosphere of epistemological uncertainty', one in which the pretension to sagacity is tempered by doubt about our own intellectual abilities.[78]

---

75   Thomas Lockwood, 'Matter and Reflection in *Tom Jones*', *ELH*, 45 (1978), 226–235 (p. 229).

76   Henry Knight Miller, 'Some Functions of Rhetoric in *Tom Jones*', *Philological Quarterly*, 45 (1966), 209–235 (pp. 230–231).

77   C. J. Rawson, *Henry Fielding and the Augustan Ideal Under Stress* (London: Routledge and Kegan Paul, 1972), p. 68.

78   Leo Braudy, *Narrative Form in History and Fiction: Hume, Fielding, and Gibbon* (Princeton: Princeton University Press, 1970), p. 11.

CHAPTER 5
THE FICTIONS OF ANCIENT HISTORY
Hume's *History of England* and the Science of Man

5.1. *Newton, Hume and the 'Science of Man'*

The very possibility of writing ancient history had long been a point of debate in Hume's philosophy. In *A Treatise of Human Nature* (1739–40), while making his argument that our assent on cause-effect relationships is a function of the vividness of the ideas involved, Hume explains that the reason one struggles to believe events that are too distant for us spatially or historically is the length of the chains of causation.[1] Given the extremely long chain of causation involved in events which occurred deep in the past, it seems 'evident' that:

> There is no point of ancient history, of which we can have any assurance, but by passing thro' many millions of causes and effects, and thro' a chain of arguments of almost immeasurable length. Before the knowledge of the fact cou'd come to the first historian, it must be convey'd thro' many mouths; and after it is committed to writing, each new copy is a new object, of which the connexion with the foregoing is known only by experience and observation.[2]

Surprisingly, Hume proceeds to claim that history represents an exception to this rule. History derogates from the problem of the long chain of causations because of the trust we put in a reliable tradition of historiographers, which is vouched for not only by

---

1   Marina Frasca-Spada, 'Quixotic Confusions and Hume's Imagination', *Impressions of Hume*, ed. by Maria Frasca-Spada and P. J. E. Kail (Oxford: Clarendon Press, 2005), pp. 161–186 (p. 166)
2   David Hume, *A Treatise of Human Nature*, ed. by L. A. Selby-Bigge (Oxford: Clarendon Press, 1981), p. 145. Henceforth 'T'.

historians themselves but also by printers. As Marina Frasca-Spada has phrased it, the transference of 'vivacity' which Hume places at the center of our assent about cause-effect phenomena in the case of history depends on mimesis, which in this context means 'the close resemblance of the however numerous links in the chain extending back in the past to the actual event'.[3] Trust in history works metonymically – the cause-effect chain may be long, but 'every single link is, on its own, enough to represent the whole multitude in our imagination'.[4]

As Frasca-Spada notes, Hume's claim amounts to an appeal to the trustworthiness of the historian. The history writer demands of his readers that they trust the narrative, and this makes historiography akin to fiction writing.[5] As Roger Maioli puts it, Hume's conception of historiography requires readers to use their imagination to warrant 'inferences from present impressions to past events', in a manner similar to how the moral contents of a novel may be pragmatically accepted by readers thanks to their imagination, notwithstanding their knowing that the events leading to them did not actually take place.[6] In other words, both the fiction writer and the historian appeal to the imagination of the reader for their claims to be accepted.

This does not mean that Hume thinks of history as a field in which imagination is to be given free rein. Imagination is to be tempered by truth, for, as stated in the *Treatise*, 'truth and reality are still requisite' in order to make ideas 'entertaining to the imagination' (T, p. 121). Timothy Costelloe observes how Hume views the human imagination as best satisfied by 'an easy transition among its ideas', which is in turn 'facilitated by the poet who inspires belief-like states with ideas that approximate truth'.[7] As Costelloe explains,

---

3   Frasca-Spada, p. 168.

4   Ibid.

5   Frasca-Spada, p. 170.

6   Roger Maioli, 'David Hume, Literary Cognitivism, and the Truth of the Novel', *SEL Studies in English Literature 1500–1900*, 54 (2014), 625–648 (p. 630).

7   Timothy M. Costelloe, 'Fact and Fiction: Memory and Imagination in Hume's Approach to History and Literature', *David Hume: Historical Thinker, Historical Writer*, ed. by Mark Spencer (Pennsylvania: Pennsylvania University Press, 2013), pp. 181–199 (p. 185).

given that any 'historical depiction' is for Hume a 're-creation, a tensed representation of experience, to which direct access is, by definition, impossible', the historian takes advantage of the Janus-faced nature of the imagination, which is responsible, on the one hand, for retaining memory accurately, and, on the other, for reproducing memories vividly, making them verisimilar.[8]

These are the grounds upon which Hayden White claims that history writing in Hume is to be assessed 'as much on literary as on scientific principles'.[9] Accurate knowledge depends on the ability to use our imagination to perceive the analogy of nature, not just in physics but also in the study of human behaviour. The reader trusts the fact that past historians related their events based on assent rather than on ungrounded conjectures, in the same way as we trust universally accepted cause-effect links. As Nicholas Capaldi observes, for Hume 'the rules of scientific procedure are the same as our natural mode of thought when the latter is done self-consciously and consistently in order to avoid the carelessness of the imagination'.[10]

But this philosophical argument finds a challenging case study in Anglo-Saxon England, an era when a reliable historiographical tradition had not yet been established. As shown in this chapter, Hume contests the veracity of the accounts of ancient historians, whom he accuses of intermingling their historical narrative with unverified fictions. But how does the present-day historian reconstruct ancient events if past historians cannot be trusted, thus disrupting the cause-effect chain upon which historiographical assent rests? As it will be seen in this chapter, the solution to this problem is a shift of the historian's craft from the study of influential men and their actions – what is critically known as neoclassical history – to a form of historiography which focuses on the study of human passions, whose regular patterns are reproduced at the level of society. Differently to the previous four volumes of the *History* on Tudor and Stuart England, which (as it will also be seen) are more focused on the sentimental proximity of the reader, in the Anglo-Saxon volumes

---

8   Costelloe, p. 187.
9   White, p. 24.
10   Capaldi, p. 42.

Hume adopts a more detached framework which seeks to exclude the will of individuals to focus on the universal laws which govern human activities, claiming in the process a degree of certainty akin to that of the mathematics-based sciences.

These claims require us to engage with the long-debated question of Newton's influence in Hume's philosophy. As a philosopher, Hume was known as 'the Newton of the moral sciences', but, as Alexander Broadie points out, several of his fellow philosophers thought themselves as Newtonians too.[11] Thomas Reid, for one, famously declared that Newton's *regulae philosophandi* presented in the *Principia* are 'maxims of common sense' which are 'practiced every day in common life' – maxims so glaringly self-evident that 'he who philosophizes by other rules, either concerning the material system or concerning the mind, mistakes his aim'.[12]

This caveat helps us get some preliminary orientation on the problem of establishing the actual influence of Newton in Hume, which is riddled with inconsistencies. James E. Force counts eleven direct references to Newton's ideas in Hume's oeuvre, but Newton's name is never explicitly mentioned in the *Treatise*.[13] Eric Schliesser and Tamás Demeter add that, although Hume was certainly familiar with Newton's ideas, in the totality of his philosophical work 'the technical details of Newton's philosophy are rarely discussed explicitly'.[14] That said, even if we were to admit that Hume had not read Newton first-hand, no definitive argument about influence should be drawn from it. Apart from mathematicians by trade, most people who were interested in Newton's ideas did not delve into the technicalities of the *Principia* anyway. For Hume to be interested in

---

11   Alexander Broadie, 'The Human Mind and Its Powers', *The Cambridge Companion to the Scottish Enlightenment*, ed. by Alexander Broadie (Cambridge: Cambridge University Press, 2003), pp. 60–78 (p. 63).

12   Ibid.

13   James E. Force, 'Hume's Interest in Newton and Science', *Hume Studies*, 13 (1987), 166–216 (pp. 169–177). On the absence of Newton's name in the *Treatise*, see also James A. Harris, *Hume: An Intellectual Biography* (Cambridge: Cambridge University Press, 2015), p. 85.

14   Eric Schliesser and Tamás Demeter, 'Hume's Newtonianism and Anti-Newtonianism', *The Stanford Encyclopedia of Philosophy* (Summer 2020 Edition), ed. by Edward N. Zalta, URL = <https://plato.stanford.edu/archives/sum2020/entries/hume-newton>.

Newton's ideas, as James Noxon and Nicholas Capaldi argued, no expertise in mathematics or astronomy was required; it was enough to be part of the intellectual climate which we have come to call Newtonianist in this study.[15]

It is hard to ascertain whether Newton's method is 'precisely' that 'which Hume claims to be following in his own thinking' in the *Treatise*, as Norman Kemp Smith claims.[16] But hints abound that some of the key conceptual premises of Newtonianism as a climate of thought were clearly reworked as part of Hume's moral philosophy. For instance, the wording of the title page of the *Treatise*, which reads 'BEING An Attempt to introduce the experimental Method of Reasoning into MORAL SUBJECTS', is telling, given that, in eighteenth-century usage, the phrase 'experimental method' was quite regularly identified with Newtonian philosophy (T, p. xi).[17] Works such as *An Enquiry Concerning Human Understanding* (1748) and *An Enquiry Concerning the Principles of Morals* (1751) then made it clear that Hume's approach to the study of humankind aimed at the same degree of certainty boasted by Newton, who is covertly referred to as the 'philosopher' who 'at last, arose' and 'determined the laws and forces' of the planets:

> Astronomers had long contented themselves with proving, from the phenomena, the true motions, order, and magnitude of the heavenly bodies: Till a philosopher, at last, arose, who seems, from the happiest reasoning, to have also determined the laws and forces, by which the revolutions of the planets are governed and directed. The like has been performed with regard to other parts of nature.[18]

Most importantly, Hume was persuaded that the standard of certainty achieved in post-Newtonian astronomy could be extended

---

15   See James Noxon, *Hume's Philosophical Development: A Study of his Methods* (Oxford: Clarendon Press, 1973), p. 28; Capaldi, chapter 3.

16   Norman Kemp Smith, *The Philosophy of David Hume* (London: MacMillan, 1941), p. 57.

17   See also Eugene Sapadin, 'A Note on Newton, Boyle, and Hume's "Experimental Method"', *Hume Studies*, 23 (1997), 337–344 (p. 339).

18   David Hume, *An Enquiry concerning Human Understanding*, ed. by Peter Millican (Oxford: Oxford University Press, 2007), p. 10. Henceforth, ECHU.

to the moral sciences. After the passage quoted above, Hume adds that 'there is no reason to despair of equal success in our enquiries concerning the mental powers and economy, if prosecuted with equal capacity and caution' (ECHU, p. 10). As Broadie and Jane McEntyre have noted, Hume believed that he was capable of translating Newton's achievements in the physical science to the moral sciences.[19] In his guise as a moral philosopher, he claimed that he could attain the same amount of certainty that animated Newtonianist endeavours in natural philosophy:

> Why do philosophers infer, with the greatest certainty, that the moon is kept in orbit by the same force of gravity, that makes bodies fall near the surface of the earth, but because these effects are, upon computation, found similar and equal? And must not this argument bring as strong conviction, in moral as in natural disquisition?[20]

5.2. *History Universalized: The Constancy of Human Nature in the History*

Commenting on the *History of England*, Hume explained that the 'philosophical spirit, which I have so much indulg'd in all my writings, finds here ample materials to work upon'.[21] As James Harris observes in his biography, Hume approached 'a subject, any subject, in a careful, analytical, and inductive manner' with the aim to derive 'general explanatory principles'.[22] On this evidence, claiming that Hume's confidence in establishing the principles of human nature with certainty was not limited to his philosophical works but extended to the *History of England*, as this chapter does, would seem a straightforward step. However, this claim clashes with

---

19   Broadie, p. 63; Jane L. McEntyre, 'Hume: Second Newton of the Moral Sciences', *Hume Studies*, 20 (1994), 3–18 (p. 15).

20   David Hume, *An Enquiry Concerning the Principles of Morals*, ed. J.B. Scheenewind (Cambridge and Indianapolis: Hackett Publishing Company, 1983), p. 53. Henceforth EPM. See also V. C. Chappell, *The Philosophy of David Hume* (New York: Random House, 1963), p. xv.

21   David Hume, *The Letters of David Hume*, ed. by G. Y. T. Greig (Oxford: Oxford University Press, 2011), p. 193.

22   James Harris, p. 19.

the scholarly prominence typically accorded to Hume's philosophy at the expense of his historiography.

Hume's works range across subjects as diverse as epistemology, metaphysics, religion, politics, economy, literary criticism and history, and such a varied output poses classificatory challenges. The standard solution has been to consider the *History* as a non-congruent, alien item in a philosophical project centred on 'epistemology and metaphysics' (as the title of an introduction to Hume's thought edited by Georges Dicker goes).[23] As recently as 2008 and 2009, two important reference books for students in need of an overview of Hume's thought offered a very limited sense of the importance of the *History of England*. In both the first edition of *A Companion to Hume* edited by Elizabeth S. Radcliffe and the second edition of *The Cambridge Companion to David Hume* edited by David Fate Norton and Jacqueline Taylor, the lion's share of the contributions is given to discussing epistemology in the *Treatise of Human Nature*, with the *History of England* relegated to something of an afterthought. In the Norton and Taylor *Companion*, the *History* is devoted one chapter out of almost thirty, as part of a conclusive group of five contributions designed to represent, alongside political theories and economic theory, the *miscellanea* of Hume's thought which fail to fit neatly with his philosophical production.[24] Radcliffe is even more radical in confining the *History* to a corner of the intellectual outlook of the Scottish thinker. In her *Companion*, declaredly 'an attempt to represent the range of Hume's ideas', most of the emphasis lies in philosophy, and on the *Treatise* especially. Hume's historiographical view is represented in the proportion of one article out of twenty-eight and as part of a sundry final section titled 'Economics, Politics, and History'.[25]

Scholars have recently taken exception to this approach, and rightly so given that half of the Hume corpus is about history (and

---

23 Georges Dicker, *Hume's Epistemology and Metaphysics* (London and New York: Routledge, 1998).

24 David Fate Norton, 'An Introduction to Hume's Thought', *The Cambridge Companion to Hume*, ed. by David Fate Norton and Jacqueline Taylor (Cambridge: Cambridge University Press, 2009), pp. 1–39 (p. 1).

25 Elizabeth S. Radcliffe, 'Introduction', *A Companion to Hume*, ed. by Elizabeth S. Radcliffe (Oxford: Wiley-Blackwell, 2011), pp. 1–18 (p. 1).

a large chunk of the remaining half is essayistic), and that Hume, differently to our modern perception, was mainly known as a writer of history by his contemporaries.[26] Particularly so in the last two decades of his life, and for a long time after his death, Hume was *the* historian, if we trust William Godwin's words in 1818 that '[w]hoever reads English history must take Hume for his text'.[27] In a national landscape that, by the mid-eighteenth century, had its most important historian in the Frenchman Paul de Rapin-Thoyras, Hume's *History of England* emerged as the most authoritative national history, and remained so until Thomas Babington Macaulay's *The History of England from the Accession of James the Second* (1848) was published. The dismissal of Hume's historical work by Macaulay himself and, before him, by the historians involved in what Mark Salber Phillips calls the 'Romantic polemic', shows that histories after Hume needed to legitimate themselves by clearing the ground from his imposing presence.[28]

Scholars such as Philip Hicks, J. C. Hilson and Noelle Gallagher have accordingly devoted increasing attention to Hume's *History*, and they have mostly done so by emphasizing its connections to traditional eighteenth-century historiography.[29] While a welcome endeavour, this attention has somewhat reinforced the prejudice, well phrased by Haskell Fain, that Hume is 'a philosopher and a historian but not both at once'.[30] However, if one considers Hume's

---

26   Donald Livingstone, 'Introduction', *Hume as Philosopher of Society, Politics and History*, ed. by Donald Livingstone and Marie Mantin (Rochester: University of Rochester Press), pp. viii–xvi (p. x); Mark Salber Phillips and Dale R. Smith, 'Canonization and Critique: Hume's Reputation as a Historian', *The Reception of David Hume in Europe*, ed. by Peter Jones (London and New York: Thoemmes Continuum, 2005), pp. 299–313 (p. 299). See also Victor G. Wexler, *David Hume and the History of England* (Philadelphia: The American Philosophical Society, 1979), pp. 90–93.

27   In Salber Phillips and Smith, p. 301.

28   Mark Salber Phillips, *On Historical Distance* (New Haven and London: Yale University Press, 2013), p. 80.

29   Philip Hicks, *Neoclassical History and English Culture* (London: Macmillan, 1996), especially pp. 170–202; Hilson, 'Historian as Man of Feeling'; Noelle Gallagher, *Historical Literatures: Writing About the Past in England, 1660–1740* (Manchester: Manchester University Press, 2012).

30   Haskell Fain, *Between Philosophy and History: The Resurrection of Speculative Philosophy of History within the Analytic Tradition* (Princeton:

intellectual biography carefully, a unifying outlook emerges, one in which the philosophical works and the historiography are the interlocked expressions of the same intellectual enterprise.

This premise is key to appreciate the complexity of the *History of England*, a multifaceted work that has been defined as a 'synthesis of statecraft, scholarship, human science, rhetoric, and philosophy'.[31] Politics in particular plays an important role, so much so that John Stewart reads the *History* as 'a political history' more so than a history of the English civilization.[32] The reason for this assessment is that Hume's historiographical enterprise is heavily oriented towards the scrutiny of the historical conditions which determined the political context of mid-eighteenth-century Britain. Coming after the tumultuous century punctuated on one end by the Civil War in the early 1640s and on the other by the Jacobite rebellion which culminated with the Battle of Culloden in 1746, the *History* can be said to have responded to contemporary concerns about 'the origins and limits of political obligation in the face of natural liberty and equality', as Andrew Sabl claims.[33]

This interpretation is particularly salient for the two Stuart volumes of the *History*, which were the first to be published in 1754 and 1757, and the Tudor England volumes, released in 1759 as the third and fourth of the series. Based on the proximity of the events included in these volumes, it has been argued that the *History* belongs to the tradition of eighteenth-century neo-classical histories. By this term, Philip Hicks means historical narratives that tried to be instructive and entertaining by focusing on events which stimulated the imagination of the reader in the way a novel would do.[34] This

---

Princeton University Press, 1970), p. 9. A similar point has been raised in Mark G. Spencer, 'Introduction', *David Hume: Historical Thinker, Historical Writer*, ed. by Mark Spencer (Pennsylvania: Pennsylvania University Press, 2013), pp. 1–12 (p. 2).

31 Andrew Sabl, *Hume's Politics: Coordination and Crisis in the History of England* (Princeton and Oxford: Princeton University Press, 2012), p. x.

32 John B. Stewart, *The Moral and Political Philosophy of David Hume* (New York: Columbia University Press, 1963), p. 299.

33 Sabl, p. ix.

34 Noelle Gallagher has drawn attention to the importance of understanding the histories of the age not as belonging to a strictly codified genre but rather as

approach to historiography is presented by Joseph Addison (in *The Freeholder*) as a set of specific stylistic choices. The best neo-classical histories are characterised by:

> that Purity and elegance of Stile, that Nicety and Strength of Reflection, that Subtilty and Discernment in the Unravelling of a Character, and that Choice of Circumstances for enlivening the whole Narration, which we so justly admire in the antient Historians of Greece and Rome.[35]

If one focuses on the Tudor volumes and especially the Stuart volumes of the *History,* Hicks's assessment is fully justified. In these volumes, Hume is keen on peppering his historical narrative with particulars that his readers could find entertaining regardless of their political views. Examples are the depictions of Charles I upon his execution, with the 'generous tear' that Hume hoped even adverse Republican readers would shed, and the description of the capital punishment bestowed upon Anne Boleyn.

The Tudor and Stuart volumes are indeed replete with episodes that owe much to the sentimental literature of the 1740s and 1750s, in that the reader is manipulated into feeling sympathy for some historical characters. Similarities have been found between episodes in Hume's *History* and eighteenth-century novels like Richardson's *Pamela* and Charlotte Lennox's *The Female Quixote.*[36] As Hume himself explains, the criteria of instructiveness and entertainment of neo-classical histories are the most appropriate to understanding the recent history of Britain on the grounds that the 'convulsions of a civilized state usually compose the most instructive and most interesting part of its history'.[37] Paired with 'instructive', the quality of being 'interesting' reproduces the classical dyad of *utile* and *dulce*, and Hume, following on in the footsteps of Clarendon's *The History of the Rebellion* (1702–1704), looked back to Thucydides

---

belonging to a porous, wide cluster of forms concerned with historiographical representation. See Gallagher, *Historical Literatures*.

35   In Hicks, p. 23.
36   Hilson, p. 217; Frasca-Spada, pp. 175–182.
37   Hume, *History of England*, I, p. 3. Henceforth 'H', followed by the volume number in Roman numerals.

and Tacitus as models for teaching moral lessons by narrating 'interesting' – that is, memorable – episodes, even if these came at the expense of chronological accuracy.[38]

Hume's originality as a historian, according to Mark Salber Phillips, consists of complementing this 'sentimental' framework with that of philosophical distance. These two 'large and seemingly antithetical frameworks' interact to convey Hume's political vision of moderation between Tory and Whig positions.[39] According to Salber Phillips, the *History* is 'a successful narrative' insofar as it encompasses 'all of British history from the Roman conquest to the Glorious Revolution' by cultivating 'a variety of ways of relating to the past, incorporating sympathy as well as philosophic elevation, actuality and vivacity as well as irony'.[40] From this angle, the goal of the volumes of the *History* was the 'intelligibility and instruction' of readers, who could be informed about divisive questions in the recent history of the country, such as that of the historical importance of the House of Commons.[41] In this sense, Hume's *History* was part of a broader project to instruct his readers on the value of moderation in political controversies, so as to overcome strife between party factions.[42]

However, that the Stuart volumes were first printed as an independent work titled *History of Great Britain*, as Karen O'Brien points out, should caution us against assuming that the whole of the *History of England* adopts the same historiographical method throughout.[43] Indeed, the volumes on Tudor and Stuart England are very different from those on Anglo-Saxon (volume 1) and Norman and Medieval England (volume 2). While in the former Hume styled his historical narrative 'by appropriating the detached yet feeling voice of the sentimental novelist or tragedian', the events of the latter volumes tended to be much more refractory to the interplay of

---

38   See Hicks, especially chapter 1.
39   Mark Salber Phillips, *Society and Sentiment: Genres of Historical Writing in Britain, 1740–1820* (Princeton: Princeton University Press, 2000), p. 47.
40   Salber Phillips, *Society and Sentiment*, p. 37.
41   Salber Phillips, *On Historical Distance*, p. 69.
42   See Wexler, especially chapters 1 and 2.
43   Karen O'Brien, *Narratives of Enlightenment: Cosmopolitan History from Voltaire to Gibbon* (Cambridge: Cambridge University Press, 1997), pp. 58–59.

sentiment and philosophy.[44] In fact, in Hume's description of Saxon and Medieval England, sentiment seems to be all but absent.[45]

The reason for the difference in method between the Stuart and Tudor volumes and the Anglo-Saxon and Medieval ones is that readers are not sentimentally involved in the events being narrated in the latter volumes, for too much time had elapsed. This difference presented an opportunity for Hume. With no risk of discontenting readers on recent historical events, the ancient history of England represented the ideal context for the 'scientific', or 'philosophical historian'. This term, which was coined by Duncan Forbes, identifies Hume's ambition to conduct historiographical enquiries in the manner of a science.[46] The science in question is the so-called 'science of man', an expression by which Hume meant that moral effects could be studied in as scientific a manner as the natural phenomena Newton analysed in the *Principia* or the *Opticks,* on the grounds that the principles of humankind are universal, and thus knowable with mathematical certainty.[47] As Hume explains:

> tho' we must endeavour to render all our principles as universal as possible, by tracing up our experiments to the utmost, and explaining all effects from the simplest and fewest causes, 'tis still certain we cannot go beyond experience; and any hypothesis, that pretends to discover the ultimate original qualities of human nature, ought at first to be rejected as presumptuous and chimerical. (T, p. xvii)

The appeal to universal principles and the rejection of 'presumptuous and chimerical' hypotheses show a strong connection to Newtonianism, as these were the principles Newton formulated in both the General Scholium and the rules of philosophy added from the second edition of the *Principia* onwards. But how does one verify such principles? This is not obvious because of moral philosophy's

---

44   O'Brien, p. 60.

45   For one, Hume refrains from expatiating on the tragic story of Joan d'Arc burned alive in Rouen. See Hume, *History of England*, I, pp. 397, 410.

46   Duncan Forbes, *Hume's Philosophical Politics* (Cambridge: Cambridge University Press, 1975), pp. 285–286.

47   Stephen K. Wertz, 'Moral Judgments in History: Hume's Position', *Hume Studies*, 22 (1996), 339–367 (p. 351).

'peculiar disadvantage, which is not found in nature', that the observer of human behaviour cannot collect its experiments as if in a laboratory – that is, 'purposely, with premeditation, and after such a manner as to satisfy itself concerning every particular difficulty which may arise' (T, p. xix). Something different needs to be done:

> We must therefore glean up our experiments in this science from a cautious observation of human life, and take them as they appear in the common course of the world, by men's behaviour in company, in affairs, and in their pleasures. (T, p. xix)

This is where the scientific historian comes into play as that who reads history as a collection of phenomena of human nature from which patterns of behaviour can be elicited. The rationale of this goal is that even across different cultural and social contexts, humankind is always the same, as Hume makes clear on a number of occasions. In the *Enquiry Concerning Human Understanding*, for example, it is stated that humans 'are so much the same, in all times and places, that history informs us of nothing new or strange in this particular'. The use of history, Hume explains:

> is only to discover the constant and universal principles of human nature, by showing men in all varieties of circumstances and situations, and furnishing us with materials from which we may form our observations and become acquainted with the regular springs of human action and behaviour. These records of wars, intrigues, factions, and revolutions, are so many collections of experiments, by which the politician or moral philosopher fixes the principles of his science, in the same manner as the physician or natural philosopher becomes acquainted with the nature of plants, minerals, and other external objects, by the experiments which he forms concerning them. Nor are the earth, water, and other elements, examined by Aristotle, and Hippocrates, more like to those which at present lie under our observation than the men described by Polybius and Tacitus are to those who now govern the world. (ECHU, p. 60)

Histories (in the plural) can thus be used as 'collections of experiments' (ECHU, pp. 83–84) on which the moral philosopher draws scientific principles, in the same way as a natural philosopher would do. This set of experiments, 'judiciously collected and compared', allows the moral philosopher to establish 'a science, which will not be inferior in certainty, and will be much superior in utility to any other of human comprehension' (T, p. xix). In Hume's view, history is the fieldwork through which the principles of moral science may be verified. History, as he puts it, is the observation of 'the phenomena of human life' (EPM, p. 57), the dataset on human life which can be used as the testing ground for the moral principles he had identified in his philosophical works.

This scientific view of history as a laboratory is clearly at work at the very beginning of Volumes I and II of the *History*. Volume I begins with Hume regretting that 'the history of remote ages should always be so much involved in obscurity, uncertainty, and contradiction' (H, I, p. 3). The uncertainty is due to the untrustworthiness of the historians of the past, 'monk annalists' driven by superstition in an age when 'the sudden, violent, and unprepared revolutions, incident to Barbarians, are so much guided by caprice, and terminate so often in cruelty that they disgust us by the uniformity of their appearance' (H, I, pp. 3–4). Hume's phrasing, with his aside on the 'unprepared revolutions' whose occurrence cannot be predicted, introduces the question of how to search for 'uniformity' in the transactions of ancient civilizations. This question replaces the search for instruction and entertainment as the cornerstone of his historiography. Even though there is no instruction and entertainment to be found in ancient times, we can still 'indulge [our] curiosity', though in a different way compared to the other ages, and with different epistemic expectations. Our curiosity about Anglo-Saxon England, Hume explains, can be indulged with '*certain* means': by looking at 'the language, manners, and customs of their ancestors, and to compare them with those of the neighbouring nations' (H, I, p. 4).

In other words, the volumes on ancient England adopt a mode of historical enquiry of their own compared to that of the rest of the *History of England*.[48] This is also asserted emphatically at the beginning to volume II on Norman and Medieval England, where Hume expatiates on the right way to write ancient history. It is the

---

48   O'Brien, p. 88.

very act of discarding unverifiable particulars, Hume contends, that makes history analogous to 'most sciences':

> Most sciences, in proportion as they increase and improve, invent methods by which they facilitate their reasonings; and employing general theorems, are enabled to comprehend in a few propositions a great number of inferences and conclusions. History also, being a collection of facts which are multiplying without end, is obliged to adopt such arts of abridgment, to retain the more material events, and to drop all the minute circumstances, which are only interesting during the time, or to the persons engaged in the transactions. (H, II, p. 4)

Ancient history, in other words, can be conceived of scientifically whenever it abridges the 'collection of facts' through the deduction of 'general theorems' and 'a few propositions'. The very expressions chosen to formulate Hume's methodology in the Anglo-Saxon volumes are significant. When readers are chronologically close to the events, 'minute circumstances' are relevant and cannot be done without; by contrast, when a long time has passed and there is no longer sentimental vicinity, minute circumstances add no value and can thus be discarded:

> This truth is no where more evident than with regard to the reign, upon which we are going to enter. What mortal could have the patience to write or read a long detail of such frivolous events as those with which it is filled, or attend to a tedious narrative which would follow, through a series of fifty-six years, the caprices and weaknesses of so mean a prince as Henry? (H, II, p. 4)

5.3. *Social Passions and the Shift from the Individual to the Collective*

With his emphasis on history as a scientific discipline, Hume displays a strong level of confidence in the possibility of making universal claims about man. In the first two volumes of the *History of England*, he attempts to have events that were 'previously recorded simply as odd phenomena' coalesce into the materials on which the science of man may be based.[49] The phenomena Hume is looking for specifically are human passions (or sentiments, the two terms being used interchangeably in Hume), which in the two *Enquiries* had been claimed to be universal to humankind. As we will see in this section, Hume's treatment of ancient history may be said to be Newtonianist in kind, in that Hume conceives of ancient history as a collection of phenomena which can inductively confirm the passions of man he had identified in his philosophical enquiries.

Passions, mixed in 'various degrees' and distributed through society, 'have been, from the beginning of the world and still are, the source of all the actions and enterprizes which have ever been observed among mankind' (ECHU, p. 60). By studying human beings as if they were 'plants, minerals, and other external objects', Hume claims that the same passions may be identified in all men regardless of the specific spatial and temporal circumstances which they lived in.[50]

> Ambition, avarice, self-love, vanity, friendship, generosity, public spirit: these passions, mixed in various degrees, and distributed through society, have been, from the beginning of the world and still are, the source of all the actions and enterprizes which have ever been observed among mankind. Would you know the sentiments, inclinations, and course of life of the Greeks and Romans? Study well the temper and actions of the French and English. You cannot be much mistaken in transferring to the former most of the observations which you have made with regard to the latter. (ECHU, p. 60)

Since human passions remain constant across all ages and places, it is methodologically possible to transpose observations made on one group of people onto another group situated in a different time and place. This is a conclusion that, according to Hume, clearly appears from both 'reason' and 'experience', two different 'species

---

49   William B. Todd, 'Foreword', in David Hume, *The History of England from the Invasion of Julius Caesar to the Revolution in 1688*, 6 vols, ed. by William B. Todd (Indianapolis: Liberty Fund, 1983), pp. xi–xxiii (p. xi).
50   Mark Salber Phillips, 'Distance and Historical Representation', *History Workshop Journal*, 57 (2004), 123–141 (p. 131).

of argumentation' that must be mastered by the writers in '*moral, political*, or *physical* subjects' (ECHU, p. 60).

The 'reason' invoked by Hume is what we would call deduction: the property by which 'considering *à priori* the nature of things, and examining the effects, that must follow from their operation', one may 'establish particular principles of science and philosophy' (ECHU, p. 121nB). Experience is the opposite faculty, that which produces knowledge 'entirely from sense and observation, by which we learn what has actually resulted from the operation of particular objects, and are thence able to infer, what will, for the future, result from them' (ECHU, p. 121nB). This is what we would call induction. In the study of human passions, as in all other sciences, reason and experience both contribute to the identification of general principles:

> Thus, for instance, the limitations and restraints of civil government, and a legal constitution, may be defended, either from *reason*, which reflecting on the great frailty and corruption of human nature, teaches, that no man can safely be trusted with unlimited authority; or from *experience* and history, which inform us of the enormous abuses, that ambition, in every age and country, has been found to make of so imprudent a confidence. (ECHU, p. 121nB)

The passions identified in the two *Enquiries* are derived by deduction; while history, the repository of data about human nature, allows the possibility of inductive verification. Crucially, whenever there is a conflict between reason and experience, the former must always be preferred. This is because experience can occasionally show 'seeming irregularities', which derive from the fact that the 'internal principles and motives' of nature are not always easily discerned by 'human sagacity':

> The internal principles and motives may operate in a uniform manner, notwithstanding these seeming irregularities; in the same manner as the winds, rains, clouds, and other variations of the weather are supposed to be governed by steady principles; though not easily discoverable by human sagacity and inquiry. (ECHU, p. 64)

It is on these foundations of commensurability that Hume challenges ancient historians and is able to reassess the history of Anglo-Saxon and Medieval England. The scientific historian evaluates historical data, discarding that which is in contrast with reason. As John Pocock argues, this part of the process is especially important to depurate the historical narrative of unreliable accounts.[51] Throughout his account of Anglo-Saxon England, Hume displays constant scepticism towards what he calls 'Monkish historians', effectively challenging their experience because their accounts are allegedly vitiated by their imagination. This point is made at the very beginning of the volume on Anglo-Saxon England. In ancient times, 'fables' were 'commonly employed to supply the place of true history', and these 'ought entirely to be disregarded' (H, I, p. 4) whenever they go counter what our reason tells us. The rationale for this claim had been explained in the *Enquiry Concerning Human Understanding*:

> Should a traveller, returning from a far country, bring us an account of men, wholly different from any with whom we were ever acquainted; men, who were entirely divested of avarice, ambition, or revenge; who knew no pleasure but friendship, generosity, and public spirit; we should immediately, from these circumstances, detect the falsehood, and prove him a liar, with the same certainty as if he had stuffed his narration with stories of centaurs and dragons, miracles and prodigies. And if we would explode any forgery in history, we cannot make use of a more convincing argument, than to prove, that the actions ascribed to any person are directly contrary to the course of nature, and that no human motives, in such circumstances, could ever induce him to such a conduct. (ECHU, p. 61)

In the science of man, one must assume a constant 'uniformity in human motives and actions as well as in the operations of body' across time and space (ECHU, p. 61). That is the reason why past historians are not to be trusted when their accounts run counter to the human passions we are familiar with. Whenever that occurs, one can conclude that ancient historians adulterated history with their

---

51   John G. A. Pocock, *Barbarism and Religion*, 6 vols (Cambridge: Cambridge University Press, 2009–2015), II, 176.

imaginations to the point that 'the whole frame of nature' seems 'disjointed':

> When we peruse the first histories of all nations, we are apt to imagine ourselves transported into some new world; where the whole frame of nature is disjointed, and every element performs its operations in a different manner, from what it does at present. Battles, revolutions, pestilence, famine and death, are never the effect of those natural causes, which we experience. Prodigies, omens, oracles, judgements, quite obscure the few natural events, that are intermingled with them. (ECHU, p. 86)

As history moves towards the 'enlightened ages', the historian sees more clearly that there is 'nothing mysterious or supernatural' in historical events but that everything can be explained by focusing on the fixed, universal laws that govern natural phenomena (such as pestilence and famine) as well as human transactions (such as battles and revolutions). To ensure that the same process applies to ancient history, the scientific historian must thus distinguish historical regularities from the fictional appendages of ancient historians. In the case of an alleged conspiracy against King Athelstan, for instance, Hume rejects the account offered by ancient sources on the grounds that:

> [t]his incident is related by historians with circumstances, which the reader, according to the degree of credit he is disposed to give them, may impute either to the invention of monks, who forged them, or to their artifice, who found means of making them real. (H, I, pp. 84–85)

Hume's point is that these historians did not conceive of human nature as having fixed universal principles, so tended to invent historical particulars whenever they needed to. This tendency to discredit ancient historians occurs every time Hume finds dissonance between their testimony and general arguments on human nature based on reason. For instance, the question of which population lived in Scotland during the heptarchy era is addressed by considering the language '[now] spoken in those countries, which is purely Saxon' as a 'stronger proof' than 'the imperfect, or rather fabulous annals, which are obtruded on us by the Scottish historians' (H, I, p. 23).

In other words, what Hume is conducting is a sustained attack against the use of imagination in ancient historiography to make up for unknown circumstances. In a manner akin to Roger Cotes's contention, in the preface to the second edition of Newton's *Principia*, that the 'true constitutions of things is obviously to be sought in vain from false conjectures', Hume accuses past historians of being poets who 'disfigure the most certain history by their fictions, and use strange liberties with truth' (H, I, p. 22).[52] The scientific historian must amend what ancient historians tell whenever their historical particulars are in contrast with conclusions 'founded on the nature of things' (H, I, p. 170).

The assessment of sentiments in society plays a vital function in the ancient England volumes of Hume's *History* because it homogenises the heterogeneous material of history, reducing events to the sentiments which caused them. Irrespective of their peculiarities, historical characters are evaluated positively whenever they make the 'interest of the body' (that is, of their society) and negatively when they fail to do so. In the former case, Hume includes all situations when a person in a position of power ignores their private interest in favour of public good. This polarisation is presented as a universal principle, one that had been first explored in the political essay 'Of the Independency of Parliament', in which Hume explains that public interest is always 'restrained by that of the individuals'.[53]

Historical characters are considered positively if they solve the tension between self-interest and public good by relinquishing the former and devoting their life to the latter. This appears clearly in those sections of the *History* with the sub-heading 'Character of the king', in which Hume offers a summary evaluation on the social achievements of each sovereign. Kings like Alfred the Great are positively assessed because their personal virtues proved beneficial to society. Alfred's 'prudence and justice' (H, I, p. 74) are the

---

52   Newton, *Principia*, p. 386.
53   David Hume, *Essays Moral, Political, and Literary*, ed. by Eugene F. Miller (Indianapolis: Liberty Fund, 1994), p. 45. Henceforth 'E'.

sentiments upon which 'his institutions for the execution of justice' were built on, and his love for knowledge stands at the basis of 'the encouragement of arts and sciences' (H, I, p. 79). When Hume writes that in Alfred's character 'happily were all his virtues tempered together', he means 'virtues' as all those passions that are positive because directed to the good of the population in general (H, I, p. 79). By contrast, Richard I, the monarch beloved by the English for the 'personal courage' and 'intrepidity' which gained him 'the appellation of the lion-hearted', is assessed negatively precisely because of such passions, which, Hume argues, were expressions of private interest and ultimately led him to become the sovereign of a reign 'very oppressive, and somewhat arbitrary' (H, I, pp. 403–404).

As examined above, the most important aspect of Hume's 'general unalterable standard' of judgment is that it holds across different times and places. Hume's confidence in identifying universal principles of moral behaviour means that his assessment of approbation or censure applies across different reigns and ages. This, as we have seen, was originally claimed in the first *Enquiry,* where Hume claimed that a historian who wants to understand 'the sentiments, inclinations, and course of life of the Greeks and Romans' should do so not by trusting ancient historians but by studying 'the temper and actions of the French and English'. Since human nature is regarded as universal, one 'cannot be much mistaken in transferring to the former most of the observations which you have made with regard to the latter' (ECHU, p. 60).

That is why an abundance of statements on the behaviour of 'mankind' are interspersed throughout the first two volumes of the *History*, especially whenever the historian needs to assess why specific political junctures came to be. These assessments are easily noticeable in the text because they are expressed in the present tense, a sign that Hume meant them as maxims to be applied regardless of time and place. For instance, the fractious relationship between King Edgar (who reigned from 959 to 975) and the Christian monks who encountered the favours of the population is explained by Hume as a consequence of the credulity of humankind: '[s]uch is the ascendant which may be attained, by hypocrisy and cabal, over mankind!' (H, I, p. 100). Similarly, assessing the frequency of civil disorders in the reign of Edward II (1307–1327), Hume refrains from pointing to causes that are specific to the historical context but finds an explanation in the proposition that 'turbulence of the great, and madness of the people' are 'evils incident to human society', which need to be carefully guarded against 'in every well regulated constitution' (H, II, p. 174). At other times, the voice of the scientific historian is manifested by carefully selected adjectives. These codify the passions of sovereigns, which, as Hume is constantly keen to specify, lead to consequences for society at large. Canute (who reigned 1016–1035) was thus 'a *wise* prince' because he 'made no distinction between Danes and English in the distribution of justice' (H, I, p. 123; italics mine), and Watheof, the earl of Northumbria (died in 1076) was 'a man of *generous* principles' because he rebelled against tyranny for the love of his country (H, I, p. 212; italics mine).

5.4. *The 'Strange Contradictions' of Human Nature: Trusting the Narrative of the Scientific Historian*

As history moves towards more modern times and the power of individuals in society gets increasingly tempered by that of society, Hume focuses on collective passions, which are exactly like those of the individual but are more regular in their workings. Based on the belief that '[h]uman nature cannot, by any means, subsist, without the association of individuals' (EPM, p. 35), Hume identifies collective passions as the chief factor affecting the course of history, with individuals being increasingly seen as manifestations of general sentiments. The earl of Glocester episode is exemplary, in that his having stirred a rebellion in 1267 during the reign of Henry III, Hume claims, was less his own doing than the offspring of the '*dangerous* independence of the barons in those ages' (H, II, p. 63; italics mine). Similarly, as Europe transitioned to the Middle Ages, collective political entities are personified by Hume as being ruled by passions. Europe is said to be subject to the 'interests and passions of the nation' (H, II, p. 156); and to explain the cause of the civil war under Henry III (who reigned 1216–1272) Hume alleges that the hostilities had been triggered by the 'insolence' of the barons as a group (rather than by a single baron), which in turn provoked 'the hatred and jealousy of all orders of men in the kingdom' (H, II, p. 9).

The argument that passions operate not merely on an individual level but also, and primarily, at a group level is what allows Hume the historian to de-particularize his historical analysis. By doing so, Hume can understand historical characters less as individuals with free will than as manifestations of group passions; and, at a higher level still, of the spirit of the age they lived in. The corruption of the catholic priests, for example, is typically seen by Hume as a defining aspect of the Anglo-Saxon and Medieval ages, a consequence which 'follows indeed, by an evident necessity', from the intellectual climate that was common to Europe at that time. It was the 'very situation' in which the 'church was placed with regard to the rest of Europe' (H, II, p. 4), Hume maintains, that led to the corruption of its clergy. In the discussion on the high number of slaves in the Anglo-Saxon age (which is included in an appendix on 'The Anglo-Saxon Government and Manners'), Hume suggests that it could not have been otherwise because:

> Great property in the nobles, especially if joined to an irregular administration of justice, *naturally* favours the power of the aristocracy; but still more so if the practice of slavery be admitted, and has become very common. The nobility not only possess the influence which *always* attends the riches, but also the power which the laws give them over their slaves and villains. It then becomes difficult, *and almost impossible*, for a private man to remain altogether free and independent. (H, I, p. 171; italics mine)

Passages like this, which are written in the present tense, once again allow Hume to present cause-effect links as principles which, because of their generality, may be applied to different ages and countries. Hume's philosophical thrust lies in the adverbs – given situations occur 'naturally' under certain circumstances and 'always' result in predictable effects. This is not to say, as Hume concedes with careful word choice, that individuals may not act contrary to the passions of the social group to whom they belong, but that it is 'almost impossible' for it to happen.

The search for general truths, and its being accompanied by a decrease in the importance given to particular actions, explains why, in the volumes of the *History* on Anglo-Saxon and Medieval England, Hume punctuates the account of the reigns of English kings with asides, digressions and frequent adjectivisation and adverbialization. These textual strategies are employed with the goal of providing a de-historicized commentary which offsets the particularity inherent to any chronological narrative. What Hume is interested in is the promulgation of general statements such as 'good morals and knowledge are almost inseparable, in every age, though not in every individual' (H, I, p. 79). Individuals, by contrast, are valuable in a scientific history only insofar as the sum of their passions reveals the overarching sentiments that characterise a group or, in some cases, even a whole age.

The problem with this categorical approach, O'Brien notes, is that it 'sits awkwardly' with some of Hume's accounts of kings and important characters.[54] The Anglo-Saxon and Medieval England transactions dealt with in the *History* are at times contradictory because men behave in ways that cannot always be readily explained by recourse to universal passions. Individuals in a position of power are especially problematical. The flow of history is heavily affected by sovereigns and important aristocrats with eccentric personality traits, which Hume struggles to account for in terms of human passions. The influential French prince Louis IX (who reigned from 1226 to 1270) is an example of a character who affected the course of history in a way that seems unaccountable in Hume's historiographical model. Louis IX, Hume wrote, was:

> a prince of the most singular character that is to be met with in all the records of history. This monarch united, to the mean and abject superstition of a monk, all the courage and magnanimity of the greatest hero; and, what may be deemed more extraordinary, the justice and integrity of a disinterested patriot, the mildness and humanity of an accomplished philosopher. (H, II, p. 40)

---

54   O'Brien, p. 88.

Here the scientific historian struggles to explain the passions of a person whose character mingles superstition and patriotism. Louis IX is at the same time a champion of liberty *and* religion even if, in Hume's view, these two passions are not compatible. Louis IX has in himself something of the monk, who is defined by *mean and abject* superstition; of the hero, who is defined by *courage and magnanimity*; of the patriot, who is defined by *justice and integrity*; and of the philosopher, who is defined by *mildness and humanity*.

The problem of understanding these complex historical characters is a vital one, for, in the history of ancient times, which is presented at the beginning of the first volume as subject to revolutions that are 'sudden, violent, and unprepared' (H, I, p. 3), the idiosyncrasies of kings and powerful nobles can single-handedly determine the outcome of important historical junctures. The disruptive presence of such historical anomalies is accounted for by self-interest. Hume, as discussed in the previous section, gives it as a principle of human nature that the interest of a group is restrained by that of individuals. It is the unpredictability of individuals that is crucial here, as their actions, being dependent on 'whim, folly, or caprice', complicate the attempt to systematise historical events scientifically. Some of the events recounted in the Anglo-Saxon and Medieval volumes cannot be easily explained because they occurred at a time when, in Hume's words, '[e]very man was thrown loose and independent of his fellows' (H, II, p. 255). In these ages, '[v]iolence universally prevailed, instead of general and equitable maxims', and the 'pretended liberty of the times, was only an incapacity of submitting to government: And men [were] not protected by law in their lives and properties' (H, II, pp. 518–522). Ancient England is described by Hume as being subject to the will of the barons, characters in whom 'so little national or public spirit prevailed', being 'so wholly bent [...] on the aggrandizement each of himself and his own family' (H, I, p. 353).

This state of affairs begs the question of whether Hume is able to consistently identify scientific regularities in ancient history, especially given his occasional exclamations that '[s]uch are the strange contradictions in human nature!' (H, I, p. 242) whenever he is faced with complex individuals – a paradoxical claim for a historian who insists on the universality of human nature. Hume first claims that he is able to treat of ancient history as a science – as Nicholas Phillipson puts it, that the scientific historian can identify a 'mental universe as regular in its operations as the natural universe described by scientists'.[55] But then, Hume also underlines the randomness of the events of ancient history, suggesting that it is only the more advanced societies which display true regularity in their workings because they are less subject to the will of individuals.

Hume's essays reveal that the problem is not so much that said principles are not at work in ancient history, but that the observer is unable to detect them. In 'On the Rise and Progress of the Arts and Science' (1742), Hume admits that the identification of general laws is 'attended with inconveniencies, when applied to particular cases', and 'great penetration and experience' is required on the part of the philosopher 'to discern what general laws are, upon the whole, attended with fewest inconveniencies' (E, p. 116), i.e., with the most explanatory power and the fewer anomalies. Nature does not admit of anomalies, but its mechanisms are sometimes too minute or remote to be apprehended, and the philosopher may struggle with determining principles. This aspect is crucial to our historical enquiries, as it appears from the essay 'Of Civil Liberty' (1741), where Hume voices his 'suspicion' that the 'world' is still 'too young to fix management truths in politics, which will remain true to the latest posterity' (E, p. 87):

> We have not as yet had experience of three thousand years; so that not only the art of reasoning is still imperfect in this science, as in all others, but we even want sufficient materials upon which we can reason. It is not fully known, what degree of refinement, either in virtue or vice, human nature is susceptible of; nor what may be expected of mankind from any great revolution in their education, customs, or principles (E, pp. 87–88)

Making this concession is equal to acknowledging the disruptive potential of history, for principles which are currently valid might be 'refuted by further experience, and be rejected by posterity' (E, p.

---

55 Nicholas Phillipson, *Hume* (London: Weidenfeld & Nicolson, 1989), p. 48.

89), thus leading to questions about previous attempts at determining the principles of human nature universally. Historical anomalies, that is, have the power of forcing the historian to revisit the principles of scientific history previously identified.

Hume's Newtonianist position that scientific objectivity may be reached in ancient history requires the reader to ignore the possibility that the principles identified by the scientific historian may be wrong due to a lack of experience. This approach is displayed via the philosopher's confidence that human nature is constant and universal. Since passions, which determine the behaviour of man, are the same in all times and places, certain knowledge can be produced about ancient history too, notwithstanding the fictions transmitted by ancient historians. By considering people as a general category rather than as a group of individuals, Hume re-conceptualizes history as a set of experiments from which general laws about human nature can be verified with a degree of certainty declaredly akin to that of mathematics-based sciences. Hume's confidence is rhetorically expressed through an emphasis upon the regularities in the behaviour of man across different spatial and temporal circumstances. To achieve this degree of certainty, however, historical characters that fail to fit into Hume's system of passions see their importance belittled in the grand design of Hume's scientific history. While this bold strategy displays Hume's belief in his ability to detect principles with absolute certainty, it also means that Hume required his readers to rely on the authority of the historian rather than just the evidence provided by historical data. In other words, for all the emphasis on the determination of moral principles, the reader must also 'trust the brushwork' of the scientific historian (in Jacob Sider Jost's apt expression) as they would do with any kind of narrative.[56]

---

56   Jacob Sider Jost, 'David Hume: History Painter', *ELH*, 81 (2014), 143–165 (p. 146).

CONCLUSION

I wish to conclude this study by offering a summary of the arguments advanced in the previous chapters, so as to take a more distanced view of the works so far analysed. The primary concern throughout the chapters of this work has been to examine a group of texts that display the traces of Newtonianism. As discussed in Chapter one, Newtonianism was relatively independent from Newton's own positions. In many cases, references to Newton were not due to a direct reading of his works, as he was considered by his contemporaries as a genial but complex writer. The commentaries on Newton all tended to emphasise that he had made an unprecedented intellectual contribution by making nature available for definitive discovery.

This position soon turned into the common assumption that Newton had been a watershed in the history not only of Britain, but of humankind. Commentators on Newtonian philosophy insisted on this point, arguing that Newton had demonstrated that nature was, and indeed should be, known with a degree of certainty akin to that of mathematics (though whether Newton believed such a degree of certainty was actually attainable is still a matter of debate).[1] Throughout this work, the term 'confidence' has been repeatedly used to indicate the belief, chiefly promoted by Newtonianist commentators, that the universal principles regulating not only nature but any other sphere, including the study of man, could be discovered with the same certainty associated with Newton's discoveries. This confidence depended on whether one was able to conform to Newton's *hypotheses non fingo*. According to this motto,

---

1   For a summary of this discussion see Kirsten Walsh, 'Newton: From Certainty to Probability?', *Philosophy of Science*, 84 (2017), 866–878 (pp. 866–867).

knowledge is certain only when it is based on the careful observation of nature, which is alone regarded as providing objective data. The only way to conduct careful observations is to avoid hypotheses, which Newton and his commentators believed to be the result of indulging one's imagination. The rationale for this requirement is that hypotheses are subjective and, as such, they cannot be verified by other observers. In other words, Newton's claim for certainty rested on the requirement that the observer of a given phenomenon does not attempt to come up with interpretations unless these were backed by verifiable data. Doing so, Newton and his commentators after him claimed, was the only way for man to produce certain knowledge.

This, in effect, meant restraining the faculty of imagination. As John Henry explains, the *hypotheses non fingo* is the synthesis of a methodology that forces man to avoid all attempts at interpretation, building on the idea that '[n]ature does not need man to make sense out of apparently occult mechanism. It just works like that'.[2] Detached from the technicalities of Newton's science, the confidence in the ability of knowing nature with certainty became a common assumption in eighteenth-century Britain, and Newton himself was transformed into a model to be emulated – what I came to call the 'ideal Newtonianist subject' in Chapter two – because of his having successfully restrained his imagination, which in turn allowed him to discover the universal principles of nature.

To appreciate how this confidence spread out to eighteenth-century prose narrative, in Chapter one I argued that it is necessary to use the term Newtonianism in a second sense that is complementary to, and a consequence of, the first, more obvious one. Together with being an extensive body of commentaries on Newton, Newtonianism is also a complex historical phenomenon characterised by the intellectual dissemination of the confidence that certainty in knowledge was within reach. While this confidence was initially emphasised in the commentaries on Newton, its links with Newton progressively weakened, morphing into a more general confidence about the

---

2   John Henry, 'Introduction', *Newtonianism in Eighteenth-Century Britain*, ed.
     by William Sweet (Bristol: Thoemmes Continuum, 2004), pp. v–xxxi (p. vii).

knowledge-making powers of man which was not necessarily linked to Newton anymore, but which became part of the intellectual landscape of British culture in the eighteenth century.

Chapter two investigated how such confidence found its way outside natural philosophy, with various traces found in moral philosophy works, poetry, and periodical pieces. The belief in Newton's 'reason' – one of the properties which codified the philosopher's ability to eschew conjectures – became so pervasive that it engendered the related anxiety that man was structurally unable to know anything with the degree of certainty that Newton had claimed for natural phenomena. This anxiety was grounded on the belief that Newton had been an exceptional man whose intellectual endeavours could not be replicated by anyone else. Confidence and anxiety, though opposite to one another, could, and often did, co-exist; writers like Addison could praise Newton as a 'Miracle' while also emphasising the inherent limitations of man's intellectual faculties, which stood out all the more conspicuously by comparison with Newton himself. The question of whether Newton, a thinker whose genius many believed had no comparison, had truly extended his 'reason' to the rest of humankind was a question that troubled many of his fellow Britons. Pemberton encapsulated this contradiction by writing that Newton had done 'honour to human nature, by having extended the greatest and most noble of our faculties, reason, to subjects, which, till he attempted them, appeared to be wholly beyond of our limited capacities'.[3] Since he furnished people with a method to discover the truth that satisfied the need for accurate knowledge, Newton was the archetypal benefactor, but he was in a sense too exceptional to be actually imitated by others.

In the three chapters that follow, Defoe's *A Journal of the Plague Year*, Fielding's *Tom Jones* and Hume's *History of England* are read as responses to the tension between the confidence resulting from living in an age in which the deepest secrets of nature had been revealed or were about to be revealed, and the anxiety that all interpretations advanced by man might be prejudiced, and thus fallacious, compared to Newton's perspicuous, imagination-free

---

3   Pemberton, 'Preface', p. 4.

reasoning. This pessimistic view finds an ambivalent expression in Defoe's *A Journal of the Plague Year*. As examined in Chapter three, Defoe's setting is that of the 1665 Great Plague, but the text is written with an eye to the possible plague contagion which threatened London from Marseille in 1720–1721. Discovering more about how plague worked was crucial for survival, and conjectures were continuously advanced by physicians to explain its workings.

Through his fictional mouthpiece H.F., Defoe rails against those who feigned hypotheses, on the grounds that doing so spread misinformation, which in turn led to a higher chance of contagion and, thus, more deaths. Throughout the *Journal*, H.F. insistently makes the argument that no conjectures on the causes of plague should be made because the disease was invisible in its operations. The problem is that no Newton was there to cast light on the workings of plague as it had been done with gravity. Eventually, in the *Journal* the only message one is able to take away from the wasteland of the London struck by the Great Plague is the awareness that avoiding conjectures is no guarantee that a better form of knowledge can be achieved. The Newtonianist confidence that nature could be known with certainty, Defoe suggests, must come to terms with the realisation that many of the secrets of nature are ultimately beyond human means, especially in extreme cases such as a plague outbreak.

The work of Henry Fielding, examined in Chapter four, enacts a tension between a marked confidence that the principles governing the behaviour of humankind could be unveiled by a 'sagacious' observer and the anxiety that man does not have the ability to see through deception. Fielding's portrayal of the 'accurate observer' in the *Essay on the Knowledge of the Characters of Men* strongly resonates with the image of Newton's 'wonderful Sagacity' that was common in those decades. The perspicuity advocated by Fielding is made necessary by the universal tendency of humankind to lie and deceive for advantage, rather than to seek truth. Notwithstanding Newton's confident assertion that, by extending his method of enquiry beyond natural philosophy, 'the Bounds of Moral Philosophy will be also enlarged', detecting truth beyond the inert realm of nature was no easy task.[4] Most people, Fielding argues, are driven by an ill-grounded confidence, and 'almost universally mistake the Symptoms which Nature kindly holds forth to us'. Indeed, 'an accurate and discerning Eye', Fielding argues, is 'the Property of the few', whereas 'the Generality of Mankind mistake the Affectation for the Reality'.[5]

Taking advantage of the liberty provided by fiction, in *Tom Jones* (1749) Fielding interprets the concept of *hypotheses non fingo* as the need to avoid being deceived by appearances when judging people who are mistakenly believed to be guilty, like the main character Tom Jones himself. Eventually, Fielding's answer to this problem is ambivalent. *Tom Jones* is constructed through two distinct viewpoints corresponding to two distinct levels of knowledge ability. One is that of the characters in the texts like Allworthy, who, notwithstanding their being described as rational observers, remain unable to see through the deception of the other characters because they are anchored to their imagination and, thus, to their own prejudices. Even though they discover the truth, there is no improvement for them – they constantly make assumptions that are proven wrong and, even worse, they never learn how to tell truth from lie because they are too confident in their being right. At a second, higher level sits Fielding's omniscient narrator, a pure body of rationality that knows how the story ends and actively engages in conversation with his readers to educate them to a scientific analysis of the behaviour of his characters. Through this double level of narrative, Fielding seems to intimate that a Newton-like sagacity could be attained. The later satirical position in *Covent-Garden Journal* on the unrealistic expectations set by natural philosophy, however, suggests that this ideal of sagacity – the ability to be unaffected by prejudices and, therefore, to discover the secrets of human nature – was one that could only be achieved in the imaginary domain of fiction. In the domain of reality, man has nothing of Newton's sagacity, and repeatedly ends up mistaking exact judgment for ill-grounded conjectures.

---

4   Newton, *Opticks*, p. 405.
5   Fielding, *Miscellanies*, I, 162.

This complex balance between confidence and anxiety, the 'sagacious doubt' symbolized by Fielding's works, would soon be accompanied by new representations offered by the commentaries on Newton. As John Henry contends, the Enlightenment image of Newtonian science emphasised 'the certainty of both the mathematical and the experimental methods' as attainable ideals.[6] The anxiety of man's ability to know nature which characterises Fielding's texts was increasingly downplayed to the point of almost complete disappearance, and the emblem of this position is David Hume, whose *History of England* is examined in Chapter five. Hume embarks in his historiography project not quite with the goal of discovering the principles of human behaviour, but by taking such principles, which he claimed to have discovered in his moral philosophy, as the initial assumption upon which even the fiction-ridden, ancient parts of the history of Britain could be rectified.

In the final two volumes of *The History of England* published in 1760–61, Hume claims that he could write the history of Anglo-Saxon and Medieval England in spite of the fact that the historical sources available were adulterated by the imagination of past historians. Hume's application of the concept of *hypotheses non fingo* to historiography is paired with a confidence in producing certain knowledge which is based on the claim that human nature is constant and universal. Since passions, which determine the behaviour of man, are the same in all times and places, certain knowledge can be produced about ancient history too. By considering humankind as a general category rather than as individuals, Hume re-conceptualizes history as a set of experiments from which principles of human nature can be verified with a degree of certainty declaredly akin to that of a science.

Hume's confidence is rhetorically expressed through an emphasis upon the regularities in the behaviour of man across different spatial and temporal circumstances. Significantly, the frequent appeals to the universality of human nature intimate that the ancient history of the English people is a metonymy for the history of humankind. The regularities found in the former owe little to the developments

---

6   John Henry, p. xv.

of English society because they are based on principles and laws that govern the passions of *all* of humankind. To achieve this degree of certainty, however, historical characters that fail to fit into Hume's system of passions are ignored, or see their importance belittled in the grand scheme of Hume's scientific history. While this bold strategy shows Hume's unshaking belief in his ability to detect principles with absolute certainty, it also means that Hume required his readers to trust the authority of the historian rather than the evidence provided by history, a position that sits uncomfortably with the Newtonian distrust of human authority endorsed by Hume.

BIBLIOGRAPHY

's Gravesande, Willem Jacob, *Mathematical elements of natural philosophy confirmed by experiments, or an introduction to Sir Isaac Newton's philosophy* (London: J. Senex, 1720).

Achinstein, Peter, 'Newton's Corpuscular Query', *Philosophical Perspectives on Newtonian Science*, ed. by Phillip Bricker and R. I. G. Hughes (Cambridge and London: The MIT Press, 1990), pp. 135–174.

Adventurer, Tuesday, March 5, 1754; Issue 139.

Alcock, Mary, *The Air Balloon: Or, Flying Mortal. A Poem* (London: E. Macklew, 1784).

Algarotti, Francesco, *Sir Isaac Newton's Philosophy Explain'd for the Use of the Ladies. In Six Dialogues on Light and Colours* (London: E. Cave, 1739).

Andrea, Alfred J., 'Mentalities in History', *The Historian*, 53 (1991), 605–608.

Atkins, Douglas G., *The Faith of John Dryden: Change and Continuity* (Lexington, KY: University Press of Kentucky, 1980).

Backscheider, Paula R., *Daniel Defoe: Ambition and Innovation* (Lexington, KY: University of Kentucky Press, 1987).

Barker-Benfield, G. J., *The Culture of Sensibility: Sex and Society in Eighteenth-Century Britain* (Chicago: University of Chicago Press, 1992).

Barnes, Harry Elmer, 'Bishop Berkeley's Essay on Moral Attraction: An Illustration of the Influence of Seventeenth Century Natural Science on Social Philosophy', *The Open Court*, 4 (1922), 251–256.

Bastian, Frank, 'Defoe's *Journal of the Plague Year* Reconsidered', *The Review of English Studies*, 16 (1965), 151–173.

Battestin, Martin C. and Ruthe R. Battestin, *Henry Fielding: A Life* (London and New York: Routledge, 1989).

Battestin, Martin C., ed., *Twentieth Century Interpretations of Tom Jones* (Englewood Cliffs: Prentice-Hall, Inc., 1968).

Beaumont, Charles A., 'The Rising and Falling Metaphor in Pope's 'An Essay on Man', *Style*, 1 (1967), 121–130.

Bechler, Zev, 'Newton's 1672 Optical Controversies: A Study in the Grammar of Scientific Dissent', *The Interaction Between Science and Philosophy*, ed. by Yehuna Elkana (New Jersey: Humanities Press, 1974), pp. 115–142.

Beer, Gillian, *Darwin's Plots: Evolutionary Narrative in Darwin, George Eliot and Nineteenth-Century Fiction* (London: Routledge, 1983).

Belkind, Ori, 'Leibniz and Newton on Space', *Foundations of Science*, 18

(2013), 467–497.

Bender, John, 'Enlightenment Fiction and the Scientific Hypothesis', *Representations*, 60 (1997), 1–23.

Bender, John, *Imagining the Penitentiary: Fiction and the Architecture of Mind in Eighteenth-Century England* (Chicago: Chicago University Press, 1989).

Berkeley, George, *Works*, 9 vols, ed. by A. A. Luce and T. E. Jessop (London: T. Nelson, 1948–57).

Blackmore, Richard, *A Discourse upon the Plague, with a Preparatory Account of Malignant Fevers* (London: John Clark, 1721).

Bowden, Samuel, *A poem on the new method of treating physic* (London: S. Chandler, 1726).

Bowers, Terence N., 'Fielding's *Odyssey*: The Man of Honor, the New Man, and the Problem of Violence in Tom Jones', *Studies in Philology*, 115 (2018), 803–834.

Boyle, Robert, *Experimental Discourse of Some Unheeded Causes of the Insalubrity and Salubrity of the Air*, annexed to *An Essay of the Great Effects of Even Languid and Unheeded Motion* (London: Richard Davis, 1685).

Bradbury, Jill Marie, 'New Science and the "New Species of Writing": Eighteenth-Century Prose Genres', *Eighteenth-Century Life*, 27 (2003), 28–51.

Braudy, Leo, *Narrative Form in History and Fiction: Hume, Fielding, and Gibbon* (Princeton: Princeton University Press, 1970).

Broadie, Alexander, 'The Human Mind and Its Powers', *The Cambridge Companion to the Scottish Enlightenment*, ed. by Alexander Broadie (Cambridge: Cambridge University Press, 2003), pp. 60–78.

Brown, Homer O., 'Tom Jones: The "Bastard" of History', *boundary2*, 7 (1979), 201–33.

Brown, Homer, 'The Institution of the English Novel: Defoe's Contribution', *Novel: A Forum on Fiction*, 29 (1996), 299–318.

Brown, Theodore M., 'Medicine in the Shadow of the *Principia*', *Journal of the History of Ideas*, 48 (1987), 629–648.

Buchdahl, Gerd, *The Image of Newton and Locke in the Age of Reason* (London and New York: Sheed and Ward, 1961).

Burke, Peter, 'The "Annales" in Global Context', *International Review of Social History*, 35 (1990), 421-432.

Butts, Robert E. and John W. Davis, eds, *The Methodological Heritage of Newton* (Toronto: University of Toronto Press, 1970).

Cantor, Geoffrey N., *Optics After Newton: Theories of Light in Britain and Ireland, 1704–1840* (Manchester: Manchester University Press, 1983).

Capaldi, Nicholas, *David Hume: The Newtonian Philosopher* (Boston: Twayne Publishers, 1975).

Carpenter, Audrey T., *John Theophilus Desaguliers: A Natural Philosopher, Engineer and Freemason in Newtonian England* (London and New York: Continuum, 2011).

Chappell, V. C., *The Philosophy of David Hume* (New York: Random House, 1963).

Cheyne, George, *Philosophical Principles of Natural Religion* (London: George Strahan, 1705).

Chico, Tita, *The Experimental Imagination: Literary Knowledge and Science in the British Enlightenment* (Stanford: Stanford University Press, 2018).

Christie, John R. R., 'Introduction: Rhetoric and Writing in Early Modern Philosophy and Science', *The Figural and the Literal: Problems of Language in the History of Science and Philosophy, 1630–1800*, ed. by Andrew E. Benjamin, Geoffrey N. Cantor, John R. R. Christie (Manchester: Manchester University Press, 1987), pp. 1–9.

Clarke, Samuel, *Sermons* (London: W. Botham, 1730)

Cohen, I. Bernard and George E. Smith, 'Introduction', *The Cambridge Companion to Newton*, first edition, ed. by I. Bernard Cohen and George E. Smith (Cambridge: Cambridge University Press, 2002), pp. 1–32.

Cohen, I. Bernard, 'The First English Version of Newton's Hypotheses Non Fingo', *Isis*, 53 (1962), 379–388.

Cohen, I. Bernard, *The Newtonian Revolution* (Cambridge: Cambridge University Press, 1983).

Colburn, Glen, '"Struggling Manfully" through Henry Fielding's *Amelia*: Hysteria, Medicine, and the Novel in Eighteenth-Century England', *Studies in Eighteenth-Century Culture*, 26 (1997), 87–123.

Connolly, Tristanne, and Steve Clark, eds, *Liberating Medicine, 1720–1835* (London: Pickering & Chatto, 2009).

Coppola, Al, *The Theater of Experiment: Staging Natural Philosophy in Eighteenth-Century Britain* (New York: Oxford University Press, 2016).

Costelloe, Timothy M., 'Fact and Fiction: Memory and Imagination in Hume's Approach to History and Literature', *David Hume: Historical Thinker, Historical Writer*, ed. by Mark Spencer (Pennsylvania: Pennsylvania University Press, 2013), pp. 181–199.

Cotes, Roger, 'Editor's Preface to the Second Edition', in Isaac Newton, *Philosophiae Naturalis Principia Mathematica*, ed. by I. Bernard Cohen, trans. by Anne Whitman (Berkeley, Los Angeles, and London: University of California Press, 1999), pp. 385–399.

Coulton, Richard, '"The Darling of the Temple-Coffee-House Club": Science, Sociability and Satire in Early Eighteenth-Century London', *Journal for Eighteenth-Century Studies*, 35 (2012), 43–65.

Cruise, James, '*A Journal of the Plague Year*: Defoe's Grammatology and the Secrets of Belonging', *The Eighteenth Century*, 54 (2013), 479–495.

Cummins, Neil, Morgan Kelly, Cormac Ó Gráda, 'Living Standards and Plague in London, 1650–1665', *Economic History Review*, 69 (2016), 3–34.

De Bolla, Peter, *The Discourse of the Sublime: Readings in History, Aesthetics and the Subject* (Oxford: Blackwell, 1989).

Dear, Peter, *Discipline and Experience: The Mathematical Way in the Scientific Revolution* (Chicago: Chicago University Press, 1995).

Defoe, Daniel, *Due Preparations for the Plague, as Well for Soul and Body* (London: E: Matthews and J. Batley, 1722).

Defoe, Daniel, *A General History of Discoveries and Improvements, in Useful*

Arts, Particularly in the Great Branches of Commerce, Navigation, and Plantation (London: J. Roberts, 1726).

Defoe, Daniel, *A Tour Thro' the Whole Island of Great Britain*, 4 vols (London: S. Birt et al., 1748).

Defoe, Daniel, *A Journal of the Plague Year*, ed. by Paula Backscheider (New York and London: W. W. Norton and Company, 1992).

Defoe, Daniel, *The Consolidator*, ed. by Michael Seidel, Maximillian E. Novak, and Joyce D. Kennedy (New York: AMS Press, 2001).

Defoe, Daniel, *Due Preparations for the Plague, As well for Soul and Body*, ed. by Andrew Wear (London: Pickering & Chatto, 2002).

Defoe, Daniel, *A Journal of the Plague Year*, ed. by David Roberts (Oxford: Oxford University Press, 2010).

Derham, William, *Astro-Theology: or, a Demonstration of the Being and Attributes of God, from a Survey of the Heavens* (London: W. Innys, 1715).

Desaguliers, John Theophilus, *A Course of Experimental Philosophy* (London: John Senex, 1734).

Dicker, Georges, *Hume's Epistemology and Metaphysics* (London and New York: Routledge, 1998).

Dobranski, Stephen B., 'What Fielding Doesn't Say in *Tom Jones*', *Modern Philology*, 107 (2010), 632–653.

Drury, Joseph, *Novel Machines: Technology and Narrative Form in Enlightenment Britain* (Oxford: Oxford University Press, 2017).

Dryden, John, *The Works of John Dryden*, ed. by H.T. Swedenberg and Edward Niles Hooker (Oxford: Oxford University Press, 1956).

Empson, William, 'Tom Jones', *Kenyon Review*, 20 (1958), 27–49.

Ermus, Cindy, *The Great Plague Scare of 1720: Disaster and Diplomacy in the Eighteenth-Century Atlantic World* (Cambridge: Cambridge University Press, 2023).

Fain, Haskell, *Between Philosophy and History: The Resurrection of Speculative Philosophy of History within the Analytic Tradition* (Princeton: Princeton University Press, 1970).

Fairer, David, 'James Thomson, *The Seasons*', *A Companion to Literature from Milton to Blake*, ed. by David Womersley (Oxford: Blackwell, 2001), pp. 284–290.

Fara, Patricia, *Newton: The Making of Genius* (London: Pan Macmillan, 2002).

Feingold, Mordechai, 'Mathematicians and Naturalists: Sir Isaac Newton and the Royal Society', *Isaac Newton's Natural Philosophy*, ed. by Jed Z. Buchwald and I. Bernard Cohen (Cambridge: MIT, 2001), pp. 77–101.

Feingold, Mordechai, *The Newtonian Moment. Isaac Newton and the Making of Modern Culture* (New York: The New York Public Library, 2004).

Feingold, Mordechai, 'Isaac Newton, Historian', *The Cambridge Companion to Newton*, second edition, ed. by Rob Iliffe and George E. Smith (Cambridge: Cambridge University Press, 2016), pp. 524–543.

Feyerabend, Paul, 'Classical Empiricism', *The Methodological Heritage of Newton*, ed. by Robert E. Butts and John W. Davis (Toronto: University of Toronto Press, 1970), pp. 150–170.

Fielding, Henry, *An Apology for the Life of Mrs. Shamela Andrews* (London: A. Dodd, 1741).

Fielding, Henry, *Pasquin: A Dramatick Satire on the Times* (London: Ed. Cook, 1787).

Fielding, Henry, *The History of Tom Jones, a Foundling*, ed. by Thomas Keymer and Alice Wakely (London: Penguin Books, 1974).

Fielding, Henry, *An Enquiry into the Causes of the Late Increase of Robbers and Related Writings*, ed. by Malvin R. Zirker (Oxford: Clarendon Press, 1988).

Fielding, Henry, *The Covent-Garden Journal and A Plan of the Universal Register-Office*, ed. by Bertrand A. Goldgar (Oxford: Oxford University Press, 1988).

Fielding, Henry, *Miscellanies*, 3 vols, ed. Bertrand A. Goldgar (Oxford: Clarendon Press, 1997).

Fielding, Henry, *The Journal of a Voyage to Lisbon, Shamela, and Occasional Writings*, ed. Martin Battestin (Oxford: Oxford University Press, 2008).

Fontenelle, Bernard Le Bovier de, *An Account of the Life and Writings of Sir Isaac Newton* (London: James Woodman and David Lyon, 1728).

Forbes, Duncan, *Hume's Philosophical Politics* (Cambridge: Cambridge University Press, 1975).

Force, James E. and Richard Popkin, eds, *Newton and Religion: Context, Nature and Influence* (Dordrecht: Springer, 1999).

Force, James E., 'Hume's Interest in Newton and Science', *Hume Studies*, 13 (1987), 166–216.

Force, James E., *William Whiston, Honest Newtonian* (Cambridge: Cambridge University Press, 2002).

Fores, Michael, 'Constructed Science and the Seventeenth Century "Revolution"', *History of Science*, 22 (1984), 217–244.

Foucault, Michel, *The Order of Things: An Archaeology of the Human Sciences*, trans. by Tavistock/Routledge (London and New York: Routledge, 1989).

Frasca-Spada, Marina, 'Quixotic Confusions and Hume's Imagination', *Impressions of Hume*, ed. by Maria Frasca-Spada and P. J. E. Kail (Oxford: Clarendon Press, 2005), pp. 161–186.

Fujimura, Thomas H., 'Dryden's *Religio Laici*: An Anglican Poem', *PMLA*, 76 (1961), 205–217.

Furbank, P.N. and W. R. Owens, 'The Myth of Defoe as *Applebee's* Man', *The Review of English Studies*, 48 (1997), 198–204.

Gallagher, Noelle, *Historical Literatures: Writing About the Past in England, 1660–1740* (Manchester: Manchester University Press, 2012).

Gascoigne, John, 'From Bentley to the Victorians: The Rise and Fall of British Newtonian Natural Theology', *Science in Context*, 2 (1988), 219–256.

Gascoigne, John, *Joseph Banks and the English Enlightenment: Useful Knowledge and Polite Culture* (Cambridge, New York: Cambridge University Press, 1994).

Gaukroger, Stephen, 'Empiricism as a Development of Experimental Natural Philosophy', *Newton and Empiricism*, ed. by Zvi Biener and Eric Schliesser

(New York: Oxford University Press, 2014), 15–38.

Gilman, Ernest B., *Plague Writing in Early Modern England* (Chicago and London: University of Chicago Press, 2009).

Girard, René, 'The Plague in Literature and Myth', *Texas Studies in Literature and Language*, 15 (1974), 833–850.

Girdler, Lew, 'Defoe's Education at Newington Green Academy', *Studies in Philology*, 50 (1953), 573–591.

Golden, Morris, *Fielding's Moral Psychology* (Boston: The University of Massachusetts Press, 1966).

Goldgar, Bertrand A., 'Fielding on Fiction and History', *Eighteenth-Century Fiction* 7 (1995), 279–292.

Gooding, Richard, '"A Complication of Disorders": Bodily Health, Masculinity, and the Discourse of Gout and Dropsy in Henry Fielding's *The Journal of a Voyage to Lisbon*', *Literature and Medicine*, 26 (2007), 386–407.

Gordon, George, *Remarks Upon the Newtonian Philosophy* (London: J. Peele, 1719).

Graunt, John, *Natural and Political Observations* (London: Martin, 1662).

Gregori, Flavio, 'Introduction: Pope on the Margins and in the Center', *Studies in the Literary Imagination*, 38 (2005), i–xliv.

Grub Street Journal, Thursday, May 20, 1731; Issue 72.

Grub Street Journal, Thursday, May 3, 1733; Issue 175.

Guerrini, Anita, 'The Tory Newtonians: Gregory, Pitcairne, and their Circle', *Journal of British Studies*, 25 (1983), 288–311.

Hall, A. Rupert, *All Was Light: An Introduction to Newton's Opticks* (London and New York: Clarendon Press, 1993).

Harris, James A., *Hume: An Intellectual Biography* (Cambridge: Cambridge University Press, 2015).

Harris, John, *Astronomical Dialogues between a Gentleman and a Lady* (London: Benj. Cowse, 1719)

Harrison, Peter, 'Newtonian Science, Miracles, and the Laws of Nature', *Journal of the History of Ideas*, 56 (1995), 531–553.

Harte, Walter, *An Essay on Reason* (London: Lawton Gulliver, 1735).

Henry, John, 'Introduction', *Newtonianism in Eighteenth-Century Britain*, ed. by William Sweet (Bristol: Thoemmes Continuum, 2004), pp. v–xxxi.

Henry, Wanda S., 'Women Searchers of the Dead in Eighteenth- and Nineteenth-Century London', *Social History of Medicine*, 29 (2016), 445–466.

Hicks, Philip, *Neoclassical History and English Culture* (London: Macmillan, 1996).

Hilson, J. C., 'Hume: The Historian as a Man of Feeling', *Prose Studies: History, Theory, Criticism*, 3 (1980), 93–108.

Hodges, Nathaniel, *Loimologia: or, an Historical Account of the Plague in London in 1665* (London: E. Bell and J. Osborn, 1720).

Hooker, Richard, *Of the Laws of Ecclesiastical Polity*, ed. by Arthur Stephen McGrade (Cambridge: Cambridge University Press, 2002).

Hudson, Nicholas, 'Fielding and the "Sagacious Reader": A Response to Lothar Černy', *Connotations*, 3 (1993), 79–84.

Hume, David, *A Treatise of Human Nature*, ed. by L. A. Selby-Bigge (Oxford: Clarendon Press, 1981).

Hume, David, *An Enquiry Concerning the Principles of Morals*, ed. by J.B. Scheenewind (Cambridge and Indianapolis: Hackett Publishing Company, 1983).

Hume, David, *The History of England from the Invasion of Julius Caesar to the Revolution in 1688*, 6 vols, ed. by William B. Todd (Indianapolis: Liberty Fund, 1983).

Hume, David, *Essays Moral, Political, and Literary*, ed. by Eugene F. Miller (Indianapolis: Liberty Fund, 1994).

Hume, David, *An Enquiry concerning Human Understanding*, ed. by Peter Millican (Oxford: Oxford University Press, 2007).

Hume, David, *The Letters of David Hume,* ed. by G. Y. T. Greig (Oxford: Oxford University Press, 2011).

Hume, Robert D., 'Fielding's *Plays* and the Completion of the Wesleyan Edition', *Huntington Library Quarterly*, 75 (2012), 447–463.

Hunter, J. Paul, *Occasional Form: Henry Fielding and the Chains of Circumstance* (Baltimore: Johns Hopkins University Press, 1975).

Hutchinson, Keith, 'What Happened to Occult Qualities in the Scientific Revolution', *Isis*, 73 (1982), 233–253.

Hutton, Ronald, *The Restoration. A Political and Religious History of England and Wales. 1658–1667* (Oxford: Clarendon Press, 1985).

Iliffe, Rob, *Priest of Nature: The Religious Worlds of Isaac Newton* (New York: Oxford University Press, 2019).

Iliffe, Robert, '"Is He Like Other Men?" The Meaning of the *Principia Mathematica*, and the Author as Idol', *Culture and Society in the Stuart Restoration: Literature, Drama, History*, ed. by Gerald Maclean (Cambridge: Cambridge University Press, 1995), pp. 159–178.

Iser, Wolfgang, *The Implied Reader: Patterns of Communication in Prose Fiction from Bunyan to Beckett* (Baltimore: Johns Hopkins University Press, 1974).

Jacob, Margaret C., 'Newtonian Science and the Radical Enlightenment', *Vistas in Astronomy*, 22 (1979), 545–555.

Jacob, Margaret C., *Newtonians and the English Revolution 1689–1720* (Ithaca: Cornell University Press, 1976).

Janiak, Andrew, 'Newton's Philosophy', *The Stanford Encyclopedia of Philosophy*, ed. by Edward N. Zalta (Stanford: Stanford University, 2016) <https://plato.stanford.edu/archives/win2016/entries/newton-philosophy>.

Johnson, Samuel, *A Dictionary of the English Language* (London: A. Millar and R. and J. Dodsley, 1755).

Jones, Peter, *Hume's Sentiments: Their Ciceronian and French Context* (Edinburgh: Edinburgh University Press, 1982).

Jones, William Powell, 'Newton Further Demands the Muse', *Studies in English Literature, 1500–1900*, 3 (1963), 287–306.

Jurin, James, *Geometry No Friend to Infidelity: or, A Defence of Sir Isaac Newton and the British Mathematicians, in a Letter to the Author of the*

Analyst (London: T. Cooper, 1734).

Kareem, Sarah Tindal. *Eighteenth-Century Fiction and the Reinvention of Wonder* (Oxford: Oxford University Press, 2014).

Kayman, Martin A., 'The "New Sort of Specialty" and the "New Province of Writing": Bank Notes, Fiction and the Law in *Tom Jones*', *ELH*, 68 (2001), 633–653.

Kemp Smith, Norman, *The Philosophy of David Hume* (London: MacMillan, 1941).

Kennedy, Peter, *A Discourse on Pestilence and Contagion in General; Containing the Cause, Prevention, and Cure* (London, 1721).

Ketcham, Michael G., 'Scientific and Poetic Imagination in James Thomson's "Poem Sacred to the Memory of Sir Isaac Newton"', *Philological Quarterly*, 61 (1982), 33–50.

Keynes, Milo, *The Iconography of Sir Isaac Newton to 1800* (Suffolk: Boydell Press, 2005).

Kickel, Katherine E., *Novel Notions: Medical Discourse and the Mapping of the Imagination in Eighteenth-Century English Fiction* (New York: Routledge, 2023).

Knapp, Elise F., 'Community Property: The Case for Warburton's 1751 Edition of Pope', *Studies in English Literature, 1500–1900*, 26 (1986), 455–468.

Knight Miller, Henry, 'Henry Fielding's Satire on the Royal Society', *Studies in Philology*, 57 (1960), 72–86.

Knight Miller, Henry, *Essays on Fielding's* Miscellanies: *A Commentary on Volume One* (Princeton: Princeton University Press, 1961).

Knight Miller, Henry, 'Some Functions of Rhetoric in *Tom Jones*', *Philological Quarterly*, 45 (1966), 209–235.

Kochiras, Hylarie, 'Gravity and Newton's Substance Counting Problem', *Studies in History and Philosophy of Science*, 40 (2009), 267–280.

Koyré, Alexandre, *Newtonian Studies* (London: Chapman and Hall, 1965).

Kropf, Carl R., 'Judgment and Character, Evidence and the Law in "Tom Jones"', *Studies in the Novel*, 21 (1989), 357–366.

Kuhn, Thomas S., 'Mathematical vs. Experimental Traditions in the Development of Physical Science', *The Journal of Interdisciplinary History*, 7 (1976), 1–31.

Landa, Louis A., 'Religion, Science, and Medicine in *A Journal of the Plague Year*', in Daniel Defoe, *A Journal of the Plague Year*, ed. by Paula Backscheider (New York and London: W. W. Norton and Company, 1992), pp. 267–285.

Lennard, Davis, *Factual Fictions: The Origins of the English Novel* (Philadelphia: University of Pennsylvania Press, 1996).

Levine, Joseph M., *The Battle of the Books: History and Literature in the Augustan Age* (Cornell: Cornell University Press, 1991).

Lewis, Jayne Elizabeth, 'Spectral Currencies in the Air of Reality: *A Journal of the Plague Year* and the History of Apparitions', *Representations*, 87 (2004), 82–101.

Lipski, Jakub, 'Defoe, Cities and the Plague', *The Palgrave Encyclopedia of Urban Literary Studies*, ed. by Jeremy Tambling (London: Palgrave Macmillan, 2022), pp. 515–520.

Livingstone, Donald, 'Introduction', *Hume as Philosopher of Society, Politics and History*, ed. by Donald Livingstone and Marie Mantin (Rochester: University of Rochester Press), pp. viii–xvi.

Lloyd's Evening Post and British Chronicle, April 17, 1761 – April 20, 1761; Issue 578.

Loar, Christopher F., 'Plague's Ecologies: Daniel Defoe and the Epidemic Constitution', *Eighteenth-Century Fiction*, 32 (2019), 31–53.

Lockwood, Thomas, 'Matter and Reflection in *Tom Jones*', *ELH*, 45 (1978), 226–235.

London Chronicle or Universal Evening Post (London, England), November 12, 1774 – November 15, 1774; Issue 2798.

Luce, A. A., 'Berkeley's Essays in the *Guardian*', *Mind*, 52 (1943), 247–263.

Lynall, Gregory, *Swift and Science: The Satire, Politics, and Theology of Natural Knowledge, 1690–1730* (Basingstoke and New York: Palgrave Macmillan, 2012).

Lynch, Deidre, *The Economy of Character: Novels, Market Culture, and the Business of Inner Meaning* (Chicago and London: Chicago University Press, 1998).

Maioli, Roger, 'David Hume, Literary Cognitivism, and the Truth of the Novel', *SEL Studies in English Literature 1500–1900*, 54 (2014), 625–648.

Maioli, Roger, 'Empiricism and Henry Fielding's Theory of Fiction', *Eighteenth-Century Fiction*, 27 (2014), 201–228.

Mallet, David, *The Works of David Mallet* (London: A. Millar, and P. Vaillant, 1759).

Manuel, Frank E., *Isaac Newton, Historian* (Harvard: Harvard University Press, 1963).

Markley, Robert, '"Casualties and Disasters": Defoe and the Interpretation of Climatic Instability', *Journal for Early Modern Cultural Studies*, 8 (2008), 102–124.

Martin, Benjamin, *A Panegyrick on the Newtonian Philosophy. Shewing the Nature and Dignity of the Science, and Its absolute Necessity to the Perfection of Human Nature; the Improvements of Arts and Sciences, the Promotion of true Religion, the Increase of Wealth and Honour, and the Completion of Human Felicity* (London: W. Owen, 1769).

Mattana, Alessio, '*Antiquitas non fingo*: Newton, the Moderns and the Science of Ancient History', *Journal for Eighteenth-Century Studies*, 43 (2020), 447–461.

Mattana, Alessio, 'The Modest Genius: Mathematics, Certainty, and the Creation of the Public Newton', *Eighteenth-Century Life*, 47 (2023), 30–62.

Mattana, Alessio, '"The Eye to the Object": The Question of Demonstrative Knowledge in Defoe's *The Consolidator*', *English Studies*, 104 (2023), 677–694.

Mayer, Robert, 'The Reception of *A Journal of the Plague Year* and the Nexus of Fiction and History in the Novel', *ELH*, 57 (1990), 529–555.

Mayhew, Robert J., *Landscape, Literature and English Religious Culture, 1660–1800: Samuel Johnson and Languages of Natural Description* (New York: Palgrave, 2004).

Mazzotti, Massimo, 'Newton for Ladies: Gentility, Gender and Radical Culture', *British Journal for the History of Science*, 37 (2004), 119–146.

McDowell, Paula, 'Defoe and the Contagion of the Oral: Modeling Media Shift in *A Journal of the Plague Year*', *PMLA*, 121 (2006), 87–106.

McEntyre, Jane L., 'Hume: Second Newton of the Moral Sciences', *Hume Studies*, 20 (1994), 3–18.

McKeon, Michael, *The Origins of the English Novel, 1600–1740* (Baltimore: Johns Hopkins University Press, 1987).

McKinlay, Alan, 'Foucault, Plague, Defoe', *Culture and Organization*, 15 (2009), 167–184.

McNamara, Susan P., 'Mirrors of Fiction Within *Tom Jones*: The Paradox of Self-Reference', *Eighteenth-Century Studies*, 12 (1979), 372–390.

Mead, Richard, *A Short Discourse Concerning Pestilential Contagion: and the Methods to be Used to Prevent It* (London: Sam. Buckley and Ralph Smith, 1720).

Miller, Laura, 'Publishers and Gendered Readership in English-Language Editions of *Il Newtonianismo per le Dame*', *Eighteenth-Century Culture*, 42 (2013), 191–214.

Miller, Laura, *Reading Popular Newtonianism: Print, the* Principia, *and the Dissemination of Newtonian Science* (Charlottesville: University of Virginia Press, 2018).

Millhauser, Milton, 'Dr. Newton and Mr. Hyde: Scientists in Fiction from Swift to Stevenson', *Nineteenth-Century Fiction*, 28 (1973), 287–304.

Moote, A. Lloyd and Dorothy C. Moote, *The Great Plague: The Story of London's Most Deadly Year* (Baltimore and London: Johns Hopkins University Press, 2004).

Morgan, Thomas, *The Moral Philosopher. Vol. III. Superstition and Tyranny Inconsistent with Theocracy* (London: n.p., 1740).

Morris, Golden, 'Public Context and Imagining Self in *Tom Jones*', *Papers on Language and Literature*, 20 (1984), 273–293.

Munkhoff, Richelle, 'Searchers of the Dead: Authority, Marginality, and the Interpretation of Plague in England, 1674–1665', *Gender & History*, 11 (1999), 1–29.

Murel, Jacob, 'Print, Authority, and the Bills of Mortality in Seventeenth-Century London', *The Seventeenth Century*, 36 (2021), 1–25.

Nate, Richard, '"Plain and Vulgarly Express'd": Margaret Cavendish and the Discourse of the New Science', *Rhetorica: A Journal of the History of Rhetoric*, 19 (2001), 403–417.

Newbery, John, *The Newtonian System of Philosophy. Adapted to the Capacities of Young Gentlemen and Ladies, and familiarized and made entertaining by Objects with which they are intimately acquainted* (London: John Newbery, 1761).

Newton, Isaac, *MS Add. 3970.3* (Cambridge: Cambridge University Library),

f. 462v.

Newton, Isaac, 'New Theory about Light and Colors', *Philosophical Transactions of the Royal Society*, 80 (1672), 3075–3087 (p. 3085).

Newton, Isaac, *Four Letters from Sir Isaac Newton to Doctor Bentley, Containing Some Arguments in Proof of a Deity* (London: R. and J. Dodsley, 1756).

Newton, Isaac, *Correspondence of Isaac Newton*, ed. by H.W. Turnbull (Cambridge: Cambridge University Press, 1963).

Newton, Isaac, *Opticks, or, a Treatise of the Reflections, Refractions, Inflections & Colours of Light*, ed. by I. Bernard Cohen (New York: Dover Publications, 1979).

Newton, Isaac, *The Optical Papers of Isaac Newton. Vol. 1, The Optical Lectures, 1670–1672*, ed. by Alan E. Shapiro (Cambridge: Cambridge University Press, 1984).

Newton, Isaac, *Philosophiae Naturalis Principia Mathematica*, ed. by I. Bernard Cohen and Anne Whitman (Berkeley, Los Angeles, and London: University of California Press, 1999).

Nicolson, Marjorie Hope, *Newton Demands the Muse: Newton's* Opticks *and the 18th Century Poets* (Princeton: Princeton University Press, 2016).

Norton, David Fate, 'An Introduction to Hume's Thought', *The Cambridge Companion to Hume*, ed. by David Fate Norton and Jacqueline Taylor (Cambridge: Cambridge University Press, 2009), pp. 1–39.

Novak, Maximillian E., 'The Unmentionable and the Ineffable in Defoe's Fiction', *Studies in the Literary Imagination*, 15 (1982), 85–102.

Novak, Maximillian E., *Daniel Defoe Master of Fiction: His Life and Works* (Oxford: Oxford University Press, 2011).

Novak, Maximillian E., 'Daniel Defoe and *Applebee's Original Weekly Journal*: An Attempt at Re-Attribution', *Eighteenth-Century Studies*, 45 (2012), 585–608.

Noxon, James, *Hume's Philosophical Development: A Study of his Methods* (Oxford: Clarendon Press, 1973).

O'Brien, Karen, *Narratives of Enlightenment: Cosmopolitan History from Voltaire to Gibbon* (Cambridge: Cambridge University Press, 1997).

Patey, Douglas Lane, *Probability and the Literary Form: Philosophic Theory and Literary Practice in the Augustan Age* (Cambridge: Cambridge University Press, 1984).

Paulson, Ronald, '*The Jacobite's Journal and Related Writings by Henry Fielding*, W. B. Coley; *The History of Tom Jones: A Foundling* by Henry Fielding', *Modern Language Review*, 71 (1976), 888–891.

Payne, Geoffrey, 'Distemper, Scourge, Invader: Discourse and Plague in Defoe's *A Journal of the Plague Year*', *English Studies*, 5 (2014), 620–636.

Pemberton, Henry, *A View of Sir Isaac Newton's Philosophy* (London: S. Palmer, 1728).

Phillipson, Nicholas, *Hume* (London: Weidenfeld & Nicolson, 1989).

Pocock, John G. A., *Barbarism and Religion*, 6 vols (Cambridge: Cambridge University Press, 2009–2015).

Pope, Alexander, *The Dunciad in Four Books* (London, 1743).

Pope, Alexander, *Poetry of Alexander Pope*, ed. by John Butt (New Haven: Yale University Press, 1963).

Pope, Alexander, *An Essay on Man*, ed. by Tom Jones (Princeton: Princeton University Press, 2016).

Power, Henry, 'Henry Fielding, Richard Bentley, and the "Sagacious Reader" of *Tom Jones*', *The Review of English Studies*, 61 (2010), 749–772.

Preston, John, '*Tom Jones* and the "Pursuit of True Judgment"', *ELH*, 33 (1966), 315–326.

Radcliffe, Elizabeth S., ed., *A Companion to Hume* (Oxford: Wiley-Blackwell, 2011).

Rawson, C. J., *Henry Fielding and the Augustan Ideal Under Stress* (London: Routledge and Kegan Paul, 1972).

Reynolds, John, *Death's Vision Represented in a Philosophical, Sacred Poem* (London: T. Parkhust, 1709).

Ribble, Frederick G. and Anne G. Ribble, *Fielding's Library: An Annotated Catalogue*, (Charlottesville: University Press of Virginia, 1996).

Richetti, John, 'Epilogue: *A Journal of the Plague Year* as Epitome', in Daniel Defoe, *A Journal of the Plague Year*, ed. by Paula Backscheider (New York and London: W. W. Norton and Company, 1992), pp. 295–301.

Ripley, Wayne C., '"An Age More Curious, Than Devout": The Counter-Enlightenment Edward Young', *Eighteenth-Century Studies*, 49 (2016), 507–529.

Risling, Matthew, 'Ants, Polyps, and Hanover Rats: Henry Fielding and Popular Science', *Philological Quarterly*, 95 (2016), 25–44.

Roos, Anna Marie, 'Taking Newton on Tour: The Scientific Travels of Martin Folkes, 1733–1735', *British Journal for the History of Science*, 50 (2017), 569–601.

Sabl, Andrew, *Hume's Politics: Coordination and Crisis in the* History of England (Princeton and Oxford: Princeton University Press, 2012).

Salber Phillips, Mark, *Society and Sentiment: Genres of Historical Writing in Britain, 1740–1820* (Princeton: Princeton University Press, 2000).

Salber Phillips, Mark, 'Distance and Historical Representation', *History Workshop Journal*, 57 (2004), 123–141.

Salber Phillips, Mark and Dale R. Smith, 'Canonization and Critique: Hume's Reputation as a Historian', *The Reception of David Hume in Europe*, ed. by Peter Jones (London and New York: Thoemmes Continuum, 2005), pp. 299–313.

Salber Phillips, Mark, *On Historical Distance* (New Haven and London: Yale University Press, 2013).

Sapadin, Eugene, 'A Note on Newton, Boyle, and Hume's "Experimental Method"', *Hume Studies*, 23 (1997), 337–344.

Schaffer, Simon, 'Newton on the Beach: The Information Order of *Principia Mathematica*', *History of Science*, 47 (2009), 243–276.

Schliesser, Eric and Tamás Demeter, 'Hume's Newtonianism and Anti-Newtonianism', *The Stanford Encyclopedia of Philosophy* (Summer 2020

Edition), ed. by Edward N. Zalta, URL = <https://plato.stanford.edu/archives/sum2020/entries/hume-newton>.

Schonhorn, Manuel, 'Defoe's *Journal of the Plague Year*. Topography and Intention', *The Review of English Studies*, 19 (1968), 387–402.

Seager, Nicholas, 'Lies, Damned Lies, and Statistics: Epistemology and Fiction in Defoe's *A Journal of the Plague Year*', *Modern Language Review*, 103 (2008), 639–653.

Sepper, Dennis, *Newton's Optical Writings: A Guided Study* (New Brunswick: Rutgers University Press, 1994).

Shank, John Bennett, *The Newton Wars and the Beginning of the French Enlightenment* (Chicago: Chicago University Press, 2008).

Shapin, Steven, '"The Mind Is Its Own Place": Science and Solitude in Seventeenth-Century England', *Science in Context*, 4 (1990), 191–218.

Shapiro, Alan E., *Fits, Passions, and Paroxysms: Physics, Method, and Chemistry and Newton's Theories of Colored Bodies and Fits of Easy Reflection* (Minnesota: University of Minnesota Press, 2009).

Sharpe, William, *A Dissertation upon Genius; Or, an Attempt to Shew, That the Several Instances of Distinction, and Degrees of Superiority in the Human Genius are not, fundamentally, the Result of Nature, but the Effect of Acquisition* (London: C. Bathurst, 1755).

Sherbo, Arthur, 'Henry Fielding. *Joseph Andrews* by Martin C. Battestin', *Journal of English and Germanic Philology*, 67 (1968), 520–522.

Sherman, Sandra, 'Reading at Arm's Length: Fielding's Contract with the Reader in *Tom Jones*', *Studies in the Novel*, 30 (1998), 232–245.

Sider Jost, Jacob, 'David Hume: History Painter', *ELH*, 81 (2014), 143–165.

Sill, Geoffrey, *The Cure of the Passions and the Origins of the English Novel* (Cambridge: Cambridge University Press, 2001).

Skinner, Quentin, *Visions of Politics. Volume 1: Regarding Method* (Cambridge: Cambridge Univ. Press, 2002).

Slack, Paul, *The Impact of Plague in Tudor and Stuart England* (Oxford: Clarendon Press, 1985).

Slauter, Will, 'Write up Your Dead', *Media History*, 17 (2011), 1–15.

Snobelen, Stephen D., 'On Reading Isaac Newton's Principia in the 18th Century', *Endeavour*, 22 (1998), 159–163.

Snow, Malinda, 'The Judgment of Evidence in *Tom Jones*', *South Atlantic Review*, 48 (1983), 37–51.

Spence, Craig, *Accidents and Violent Death in Early Modern London, 1650–1750* (Woodbridge: The Boydell Press, 2016).

Sprat, Thomas, *The history of the Royal-Society of London for the improving of natural knowledge* (London: J. Martyn and J. Allestry, 1667).

Stark, Ryan J., *Rhetoric, Science, and Magic in Seventeenth-Century England* (Washington: The Catholic University of America Press, 2009).

Stewart, John B., *The Moral and Political Philosophy of David Hume* (New York: Columbia University Press, 1963).

Stewart, Larry, *The Rise of Public Science: Rhetoric, Technology, and Natural Philosophy in Newtonian Britain, 1660–1750* (Cambridge: Cambridge

University Press, 1992).

Striner, Richard, 'Political Newtonianism: The Cosmic Models of Politics in Europe and America', *The William and Mary Quarterly*, 52 (1995), 583–608.

Sullivan, Erin, 'Physical and Spiritual Illness. Narrative Appropriations of the Bills of Mortality', *Representing the Plague in Early Modern England*, ed. by Rebecca Totaro and Ernest B. Gilman (London: Routledge, 2011), pp. 76–94.

Swenson, Rivka, 'Optics, Gender, and the Eighteenth-Century Gaze: Looking at Eliza Haywood's Anti-Pamela', *The Eighteenth Century*, 51 (2010), 27–43.

Teeter Dobbs, Betty Jo, *The Janus Faces of Genius: The Role of Alchemy in Newton's Thought* (Cambridge: Cambridge University Press, 2003).

The Covent-Garden Journal, Saturday, November 11, 1752; Issue 70.

The Spectator, Saturday, November 22, 1712; Issue 543.

The Spectator, Friday, July 9, 1714; Issue 565.

Thompson, Helen, '"It was Impossible to Know These People": Secondary Qualities and the Form of Character in *A Journal of the Plague Year*', *The Eighteenth Century*, 54 (Summer, 2013), 153–167.

Tindal Kareem, Sarah, *Eighteenth-Century Fiction and the Reinvention of Wonder* (Oxford: Oxford University Press, 2014).

Todd, William B., 'Foreword', in David Hume, *The History of England from the Invasion of Julius Caesar to the Revolution in 1688*, 6 vols, ed. by William B. Todd (Indianapolis: Liberty Fund, 1983), pp. xi–xxiii.

Toker, Leona, *Eloquent Reticence: Withholding Information in Fictional Narrative* (Lexington, KY: University Press of Kentucky, 1993).

Totaro, Rebecca, 'Introduction', *Representing the Plague in Early Modern England*, ed. by Rebecca Totaro and Ernest B. Gilman (New York and London: Routledge, 2010), pp. 1–15.

Twombly, David J., 'Newtonian Schemes: An Unknown Poetic Satire from 1728', *British Journal for Eighteenth-Century Studies*, 28 (2005), 251–272.

Universal Spectator and Weekly Journal, Saturday, March 23, 1745; Issue 859.

Vermij, Rienk, 'The Formation of the Newtonian Philosophy: The Case of the Amsterdam Mathematical Amateurs', *British Journal for the History of Science*, 36 (2003), 183–200.

Vickers, Ilse, *Defoe and the New Sciences* (Cambridge: Cambridge University Press, 1996).

Voltaire, François-Marie Arouet de, *Letters Concerning the English Nation* (London: C. Davis and A. Lyon, 1733.

Voltaire, François-Marie Arouet de, *The Elements of Sir Isaac Newton's Philosophy. Translated from the French* (London: Stephen Austen, 1737).

Wainwright, W. L., 'Lending to the Lord: Defoe's Rhetorical Design in *A Journal of the Plague Year*', *British Journal for Eighteenth-Century Studies*, 13 (1990), 59–72.

Walsh, Kirsten, 'Newton: From Certainty to Probability?', *Philosophy of Science*, 84 (2017), 866–878.

Warburton, William, *A Vindication of Mr. Pope's Essay on Man, from the Misrepresentations of Mr de Crousaz* (London: J. Robinson, 1740).

Warner, John M., 'The Interpolated Narratives in the Fiction of Fielding and Smollett: An Epistemological View', *Studies in the Novel*, 5 (1973), 271–283.

Weiss Smith, Courtney, *Empiricist Devotions: Science, Religion, and Poetry in Early Eighteenth-Century England* (Charlottesville: University of Virginia Press, 2016).

Wertz, Stephen K., 'Moral Judgments in History: Hume's Position', *Hume Studies*, 22 (1996), 339–367.

West, John, *Dryden and Enthusiasm: Literature, Religion and Politics in Restoration England* (Oxford: Oxford University Press, 2018).

Westfall, Richard S., *Never at Rest: A Biography of Isaac Newton* (Cambridge: Cambridge University Press, 1980).

Wexler, Victor G., *David Hume and the History of England* (Philadelphia: The American Philosophical Society, 1979).

Whiston, William, *New Theory of the Earth* (London: Benj. Tooke, 1696).

Whiston, William, *Sir Isaac Newton's Mathematick Philosophy More Easily Demonstrated* (London: J. Senex, 1716).

White, Hayden, 'The Fictions of Factual Representation', *Grasping the World: The Idea of the Museum*, ed. by Donald Preziosi and Claire Farago (Abingdon and New York: Routledge, 2018), pp. 22–34.

Whitehall Evening Post or London Intelligencer, April 12, 1750 – April 14, 1750; Issue 651.

Wigelsworth, Jeffrey R., 'Lockean Essences, Political Posturing, and John Toland's Reading of Isaac Newton's *Principia*', *Canadian Journal of History*, 38 (2003), 521–535.

Wild, Wayne, '"Due Preparations": Defoe, Dr Mead and the Threat of Plague', *Liberating Medicine, 1720–1835*, ed. by Tristanne Connolly and Steve Clark (London: Pickering & Chatto, 2009), pp. 55–69.

Willan, Claude, 'The Proper Study of Mankind in Pope and Thomson', *ELH*, 84 (2017), 63–90.

Wilner, Arlene, 'Henry Fielding and the Knowledge of Character', *Modern Language Studies*, 18 (1988), 181–194.

Wilner, Arlene, 'The Mythology of History, the Truth of Fiction: Henry Fielding and the Cases of Bosavern Penlez and Elizabeth Canning', *The Journal of Narrative Technique*, 21 (1991), 185–201.

Wing Lau, Travis Chi, 'Defoe Before Immunity: A Prophylactic *Journal of the Plague Year*', *Digital Defoe: Studies in Defoe & His Contemporaries*, 8 (2016), 23–39.

Young, B. W., '"See Mystery to Mathematics Fly": Pope's *Dunciad* and the Critique of Religious Rationalism', *Eighteenth-Century Studies*, 26 (1993), 435–448.

Young, Edward, *The Consolation. Containing, Among Other Things, I. A Moral Survey of the Nocturnal Heavens. II. A Night-Address to the Deity* (London: G. Hawkins, 1745).

Zimmerman, Everett, *The Boundaries of Fiction* (Ithaca and London: Cornell University Press, 1996).
Zuckerman, Arnold, 'Plague and Contagionism in Eighteenth-Century England: The Role of Richard Mead', *Bulletin of the History of Medicine*, 78 (2004), 273–308.

Printed by
Rotomail Italia S.p.A.
October 2024